The Presidential Contest

The Presidential Contest
With a Guide to the
1988 Presidential Race

Third Edition

Richard A. Watson
University of Missouri—Columbia

A Division of Congressional Quarterly Inc.
1414 22nd Street N.W., Washington, D.C. 20037

Cover Photo: Gary Garrison

Library of Congress Cataloging-in-Publication Data

Watson, Richard Abernathy, 1923-
    The presidential contest.

    Bibliography: p.
    Includes index.
    1. Presidents—United States—Election.   I. Title.
JK524.W38   1988   324.973′ 092   87-22289
ISBN 0-87187-439-3

To the memory of
Hubert Horatio Humphrey

Contents

Preface   xi
Introduction   1

1 Nomination Rules and Candidates   5

Evolution of the Nomination Process   6
Current Nomination Rules   9
The Pool of Candidates   20
Notes   27
Selected Readings   28

2 The Nomination Campaign   29

Early Maneuvering   30
Targeting the Nomination Campaign   34
Manipulating Political Appeals   38
Communicating Political Appeals   43
Campaign Organization and Workers   45
Campaign Finance   47
Summary of Developments in Recent
   Nomination Campaigns   49
The National Convention   50
Notes   57
Selected Readings   58

3 Election Rules and the Election Campaign   59

Rules of the Election Contest   59
The General Election Campaign   67

Contents

Notes 88
Selected Readings 90

4 Voting in Presidential Elections   91

Participation in Presidential Elections 91
Voting Preferences in Presidential Elections 98
Consequences of Presidential Elections 109
Notes 116
Selected Readings 118

5 Summary and Assessment of Presidential Contests   119

The Nomination of the President 119
The Election of the President 121
Notes 128

Appendixes: Guide to the 1988 Presidential Race   131

A: Schedule of 1988 Presidential Primaries
  and Caucuses 133
B: Profiles of Major Candidates in the 1988
  Presidential Contest 135
C: Results of Presidential Contests, 1932-1980 143

Index 149

Tables and Figures ═══════════════

Tables

2-1 Leading Presidential Candidates and Nominees,
    1936-1984   35
2-2 Major Candidates for 1984 Democratic Nomination   40
3-1 Cost of Presidential General Elections, 1940-1972   68
4-1 Participation of General Public in Presidential
    Elections, 1932-1984   95
4-2 Participation of Various Groups in Presidential
    Elections, 1972-1984   96
4-3 Party Identification, 1952-1984   99
4-4 Group Voting Patterns in Presidential Elections,
    1952-1984   102

Figures

1-1 Delegate Selection Methods by State and Region, 1984   13
2-1 Cumulative Proportions of Each Democratic Candidate's
    Total Expenditures and Delegates Apportioned over Time,
    1983-1984   48
3-1 State Size by Number of Electoral Votes, 1984   65
4-1 Appeal of Democratic and Republican Candidates for
    President, 1952-1980   105

Tables and Figures

Preface

This book presents a concise yet thorough account of the many aspects of the presidential contest. It treats all stages of the selection of the president, from the beginning of the quest long before the election year to the final vote in November.

A chronological, step-by-step analysis and a common framework enable the reader to see both the similarities and the differences between the nomination and election phases of the contest. The book also provides an in-depth analysis of the voters in presidential elections—who they are, why they vote as they do, and the consequences of that voting for the political party system and for policy making in the United States. The concluding chapter summarizes and assesses the strengths and weaknesses of the presidential selection process and suggests reforms for improving that process.

The Presidential Contest should be useful as a supplementary text in regular college courses—such as American Government, Political Parties, and the American Presidency—as well as in special election-year courses dealing with the selection of the president. It also should be helpful to journalists, politicians, and citizens both in this country and abroad who are interested in gaining a better understanding of the American presidential contest.

This revision of the book incorporates findings from many excellent studies of the presidential contest that have been published since the second edition. It covers all aspects of the 1984 race as well as developments in the initial phases of the 1988 contest.

I appreciate the assistance of many people with this edition, especially my students in the American Presidency and Political Parties courses who have forced me to think through the complicated rules that govern presidential contests and the political factors that shape the strategies and results of such contests. Rhodes Cook and Phil Duncan of Congressional Quarterly provided me with information on the 1988 state caucuses and primaries. And for again doing exceptional work, I thank Joanne D. Daniels, Margaret Seawell Benjaminson, and Noell Sottile—the highly efficient CQ Press team who handled *The Politics of the Presidency,* a larger work by Norman C. Thomas and me, from which this book is drawn.

Richard A. Watson

Introduction ⎯⎯⎯⎯⎯⎯⎯⎯⎯⎯⎯⎯

In a democratic society, elections are the principal means by which those "outside" the government pass judgment on those "inside" the government. Periodically, major officeholders are required to come before the populace to renew their right to exercise political power. Also part of the system are the one or more alternative groups of leaders whom voters can elect if they are dissatisfied with the performance of those currently in office. As Joseph Schumpeter observed, in a democracy individuals acquire the right to make political decisions by means of a "competitive struggle for the people's vote." [1]

This "competitive struggle" is a continuous process as leaders in and out of power attempt to convince the voters that under their particular administration the public would fare better.[2] The major effort to win over the electorate, however, is concentrated in the period immediately before the election. During this time, candidates mount campaigns using a variety of political appeals designed to motivate the general public to take the time and effort to vote, and to vote for them.

According to democratic theory, political campaigns and elections perform several important functions in society. As Stephen Hess points out, they are primarily a process of "personnel selection," with the electorate operating as a "gigantic search committee" for the nation's political leaders.[3] However, campaigns and elections also serve other purposes. As previously indicated, they offer a "corrective" for past electoral mistakes—the chance to "throw the rascals out" and to give a new team the opportunity to govern the nation. Campaigns also enable candidates to identify the principal problems in a society and to propose policies and programs for dealing with such problems; viewed in this way, campaigns are "educational," a basic civics lesson for the electorate. The electoral process can also be a catharsis, enabling societal conflicts to be made public and thereby better faced. Such a process may lead to

1

another function of democratic elections: development of attitudes of political compromise and the furthering of social consensus.[4]

Although elections of major public officials are important in any democratic society, they are especially so in the United States because of its presidential form of government. Under the parliamentary system used in most other democracies in the world, the voters do not directly choose the nation's executive officials. Instead they choose the members of the legislative body, who bargain with one another over the composition of the cabinet, including its leader, usually called the prime minister. But in the United States, the presidential election is separate from legislative contests, so that voters pass judgment directly on the candidates for the nation's highest office. In addition, because the United States has a two-party instead of a multiparty system, most of the votes go to the two major candidates, with the winner generally receiving a significant percentage of the total popular vote.[5]

Another distinguishing feature of U.S. presidential contests is the significant role the voters play in the *nomination* of candidates for the nation's highest office. In most other democratic societies, political party leaders, acting through committees or conferences, choose persons to represent them in the general election. In the United States, the two principal parties use national conventions composed of delegates from all the states to select their candidates. As indicated in Chapter 1, however, the choice of these delegates in recent years has been vested more and more in rank-and-file voters instead of traditional party activists. As a result, the nomination as well as the election of the president have become a contest in which candidates must establish their popularity with the average voter.

These reasons—along with the important powers of the office—make the contest for the U.S. presidency the most significant democratic election in the world. In no other country do so many voters cast their ballot directly for a single officeholder. Nowhere else does a single political campaign last as long and involve as many people or the expenditure of so much money. No other electoral contest receives as much coverage from the mass media. By any standard, a U.S. presidential contest is the "World Series" of electoral politics.

The following chapters trace the presidential contest from its earliest beginnings to its culmination on election day in early November. Chapter 1 provides background information on the rules of the nomination process, the ways they have evolved over the years, and their current nature and impact. It also discusses the pool of candidates from which the voters draw their presidential aspirants. Chapter 2 analyzes the nomination campaign itself—the early maneuvering for position, the targeting of the primary and caucus-convention states, the manipulation of political appeals, the communication of those appeals through the media and campaign workers, the handling of campaign finances, and the ultimate decision—the selection of the presidential and vice-presidential candidates by the parties' national conventions.

Chapter 3 shifts to the general election, analyzing it in the same framework that was used for the nomination process. This enables the reader to see the similarities and differences in the two distinct phases of the presidential contest. Chapter 4, which deals with voting in presidential elections, first traces the progressive extension of the franchise to more and more Americans and then analyzes the extent to which persons have actually exercised their right to vote in recent elections. The chapter then examines the effect of political party affiliation, social group and class identification, candidate appeal, issues, events, and presidential performance on the voting decisions of the American people. The concluding section of the chapter analyzes the consequences of presidential elections for the political party system and for policy making in the United States.

These four chapters thus chronicle the entire presidential contest, reporting and integrating a wide variety of studies of the subject. Chapter 5 is more in the form of an extended essay or editorial; it is a personal assessment of what is right and wrong about the way the nation's highest political official is chosen and what can be done to improve the process.

The appendixes contain supplemental information on the presidential contest. Appendix A is a schedule of the 1988 primaries and caucuses; Appendix B contains profiles of the major candidates for the 1988 contest; and Appendix C shows the results of presidential contests from 1932 through 1984.

Notes

1. Joseph Schumpeter, *Capitalism, Socialism, and Democracy,* 3d ed. (New York: Harper and Row, 1950), 269.
2. As discussed in Chapter 4, the concept of the "people's vote" has changed over the years in the United States as the franchise has been extended to more and more groups; this trend toward broader public participation is also a feature of democratic elections.
3. Stephen Hess, *The Presidential Campaign* (Washington, D.C.: Brookings, 1974), chap. 4.
4. Morris Janowitz and Dwaine Marvick, *Competitive Pressure and Democratic Consent* (Ann Arbor, Michigan: Bureau of Government, Institute of Public Administration, 1956), 2.

5. The winning presidential candidate must receive a majority of the votes in the electoral college. (See Chapter 3.) Since the Civil War, the winner in the electoral college has always received at least 40 percent of the popular vote and usually has received more than 50 percent of that vote.

Nomination Rules and Candidates 1

Persons who seek the presidency today must pass through a long and complicated process by which Americans test aspirants for the nation's highest office. Moreover, they must survive two separate tests of political strength. First, candidates must win their party's nomination for the presidency; then, they must emerge victorious in the general election over the major party rival.

These two phases of the presidential contest not only lengthen the electoral process but also require candidates to wage two separate campaigns. The rules for the nomination and election contests are quite different. Moreover, campaign strategies and techniques must be tailored for the two distinct stages of the presidential battle. Finally, the participants in the two contests are not the same: Hugh Heclo has labeled those who help choose presidential nominees as the "selectorate," in contrast to the "electorate," who vote in the general election.[1]

The characteristic nomination and election phases of the presidential contest have developed over the course of U.S. political history. The Founders never contemplated this separation in the procedure they devised for choosing the chief executive. Major developments in the young nation soon resulted, however, in the division of the selection process into two parts. Moreover, after the process became divided, changes continued to occur in both the nomination and election of the president.

This chapter first describes the development of the nomination process, from the establishment of the congressional caucus in 1796 until the national convention system was instituted in the 1830s and expanded in the 1840s. It then shifts to an explanation of the nature and impact of current nomination rules. The final section analyzes the backgrounds of presidential candidates.

Evolution of the Nomination Process

During the nation's first seven years, from 1789 to 1796, there was no separate procedure for nominating the president. The system operated as the Founders intended: members of the political elite from the various states, acting through the mechanism of the electoral college (see Chapter 3), chose George Washington to lead the country in 1789 and again in 1792. Persons with diverse political views agreed that the nation's wartime hero was a "patriot king" who would rule in the interest of all the people.

In Congress, however, no such political consensus prevailed. In 1790 Alexander Hamilton, the first secretary of the treasury in the Washington administration, presented an economic program that would establish a national bank and a tariff to protect U.S. manufacturers and merchants from foreign competition. Thomas Jefferson, then secretary of state, and James Madison, a member of Congress, opposed the program on the grounds that it benefited only mercantile interests and not the nation's farmers, for whom they had great admiration. Subsequently, Jefferson and Madison also differed with Hamilton on the Jay Treaty, negotiated with England in 1794. Under its terms the British agreed, among other things, to withdraw troops from forts in the Northwest. The treaty failed to satisfy, however, two other grievances of concern to Jefferson and Madison: the lack of compensation for slaves carried away by British soldiers during the Revolution and the impressment into the British Navy of U.S. sailors from U.S. ships seized by the British for trading with the French (who were at war with Britain).

Out of these controversies over domestic and foreign policy emerged an important institution not provided for by the U.S. Constitution— political parties. The Federalist party had formed by the early 1790s with Hamilton acting as the principal initiator of policies in Congress and Washington as the popular leader who could rally support for such policies. Federalists soon were running for Congress and, once in office, voting for Hamilton's programs.[2] Jefferson's resignation from the Washington administration in 1793 and Madison's congressional disputes with Hamilton paved the way for a rival political party, the Republicans.[3] By the mid-1790s cohesive pro- and antiadministration blocs were voting against each other in Congress, and congressional candidates were being identified as Republicans as well as Federalists.[4] George Washington's retirement at the end of his second term in 1797 created an opening for party politics, which then spread from Congress to the presidency.

The creation of political parties in the United States thus ended the brief period in which the political elite of the day selected the president.

From then on, party politics would determine the nation's chief executive. This development required the parties to devise some means of choosing candidates to run under their party name, a process known as *nomination*. In 1796 the Federalists chose their candidate, John Adams, through consultation among their prominent leaders. The Republicans turned to their party members in Congress, who nominated Thomas Jefferson as their standard-bearer. Four years later the Federalists followed suit, and the congressional caucus became the nominating mechanism for both parties.

Congressional Caucuses

The congressional caucus was quite practical in this early stage of party development. Because members of Congress were already assembled in the nation's capital, they faced no transportation problems. Moreover, the nominating task was manageable among so few members. They also were quite knowledgeable about potential presidential candidates from all parts of the new country and so were logical agents for choosing candidates for the presidency with its nationwide constituency.

The congressional caucus had serious defects, however. First, it violated the separation-of-powers principle of the Constitution, because members of the legislative body played a key role in choosing the president. Second, the caucus failed to represent areas in which the party had lost the previous congressional election. In addition, interested and informed citizens who participated in grass-roots party activities (especially campaigns) took no part in the deliberations of the congressional caucus.

In time these flaws undermined the congressional caucus system. The Federalists were the first to be affected. As their political fortunes waned, the size of the party's congressional delegation declined so much that it was no longer a viable and representative body. The party was forced to turn to alternative nominating devices. In 1808 and 1812 the Federalists gathered in what one political scientist calls "primitive national conventions," meetings of state delegates closed to persons not specifically invited (only about half the states were represented).[5] In 1816, the party held no organized caucus or convention; instead, it chose its nominee by common consent.[6] The 1816 presidential election was the last contested by the Federalists. The party had lost public support because of internal divisions, failure to organize grass-roots interests, and the pro-British attitude of many of its leaders during the War of 1812. The Republicans had a quite different experience with the congressional caucus. Between 1800 and 1820 the party nominated three Virginians

7

who had previously served as secretary of state: Jefferson was the nominee in 1800 and 1804, Madison in 1808 and 1812, and James Monroe in 1816 and 1820. However, when the Republican congressional caucus attempted in 1824 to nominate Secretary of the Treasury William Crawford (even though he was from Georgia, he was Virginian by birth), three-fourths of the Republican members of Congress boycotted the meeting.

Eventually, five candidates were nominated (principally by state legislatures) for president in 1824, including Andrew Jackson, who was proposed by the Tennessee legislature. In the election Jackson won more popular votes than any other candidate, but no candidate received a majority of the electoral votes; as a result, the election was thrown into the House of Representatives. The House, however, did not choose Jackson but awarded the presidency to John Quincy Adams (also a former secretary of state). Adams had benefited from a political deal with Henry Clay, one of the five nominees, who gave his House support to Adams in return for being named secretary of state. This unfortunate combination of circumstances discredited the congressional caucus (by then known as "King Caucus") as a means of nominating presidential candidates.

In 1828 responsibility for presidential nominations was vested entirely in the states, where legislatures and conventions chose "favorite sons" such as Jackson and Adams as candidates. Although the congressional caucus was too centralized to represent the state and local party units, the individual states were too decentralized to select a national official. Some device was needed that would represent party elements throughout the country and at the same time facilitate the nomination of a common candidate.

National Party Conventions

The nomination method that emerged to meet these needs was a genuine national party convention composed of delegates from all the states. A minor party, the Anti-Masons, pioneered the way in 1831 by convening such an assembly. The National Republicans called a similar convention the following year.[7] (Like the Anti-Masons, the National Republicans had no appreciable representation in Congress and thus could not have used the congressional caucus even if they had wanted to.) The Democratic-Republicans, under President Jackson (elected in 1828), also held a convention in 1832. Jackson viewed the convention as an ideal way of securing the vice-presidential nomination for his handpicked candidate, Martin Van Buren.

Since the early 1840s, major political parties have nominated their presidential and vice-presidential candidates by holding national conventions. Since the early 1850s, national committees have called the presidential nominating conventions into session, and conventions have adopted a platform.[8] As will be discussed later, today's parties retain in modified form two of the basic features of the early conventions: the allocation of delegates to states primarily on the basis of their representation in Congress (senators plus House members), and the selection of delegates by each state.

Although today's nominating conventions resemble those that developed almost 150 years ago, the entire nomination process has undergone drastic change, especially since 1968. The next section of this chapter focuses on the current rules governing the nomination of candidates.

Current Nomination Rules

The rules that govern any political contest are important. Rules both prescribe behavior in political contests and influence election outcomes. By determining the strategies and tactics that participants adopt to improve their chances of winning, rules shape the nominating process. Yet they are shaped by the process as well. As people seek advantage for their particular interests, rules become the focus of struggles for change. The prevailing rules are seldom neutral: they inevitably favor some individuals and interests over others—sometimes by design, sometimes not.

Since the late 1960s the rules of the presidential nomination contest have become especially important. They are highly complicated because they come from a variety of sources—100 state political parties and 50 legislatures, the national political parties, and the Congress. (Sometimes individuals also turn to the courts to interpret provisions of these regulations and to reconcile conflicts among them.) In addition, the rules have been changed so drastically and so often, particularly in the Democratic party, that it is difficult for candidates and their supporters to keep up with the changes. These changes have created confusion and uncertainty for many participants and have favored those who somehow manage to puzzle their way through the welter of rules. Indeed, some persons contend that Sen. George McGovern won the 1972 Democratic nomination partly because of his close association with the changes made in the nomination rules of that year. (As discussed later in this chapter, McGovern originally chaired the commission that helped bring about changes in the 1972 nomination contest.)

Many rules govern the different stages of the nomination process. The following three sections examine the rules for apportioning convention delegates among the states, selecting delegates within the states, and financing nomination campaigns.

Allocating National Convention Delegates

A presidential candidate starts out with a well-defined goal: to win a majority of the votes at the party's national convention in order to be nominated for the presidency. At the conventions in 1984, the Republican nominee had to win 1,118 votes out of 2,235; the Democratic nominee, 1,967 out of 3,933.

Although the numbers of their convention votes differ, both parties use the same general formulas to decide how many votes each state is entitled to cast at the convention. The parties take into account the size of a state's congressional delegation or its population in determining its basic vote allocation, and its record in supporting the party's candidates in recent years in allocating extra, or "bonus," votes to each state. The methods that parties use to determine these bonus votes benefit some states at the expense of others.

The Republican party is interested in a state's recent voting record not only for the presidential nominee but also for governors, senators, and representatives; however, it does not take into account the *size* of the popular vote for these officials, simply whether or not they win. The smaller states, especially those in which the Republican party dominates the nonpresidential elections, therefore have a disproportionate influence in the GOP (Grand Old Party) convention. For example, a state with a small population that has elected a large number of Republican officials, such as Utah, is benefited, even though its small size means that it can cast relatively few popular votes for Republican candidates for president. A large two-party state such as New York, however, is at a disadvantage. Democratic candidates may win elections for governor, U.S. senator, or U.S. representative, which costs the state Republican party bonus votes at the convention; and the large number of popular votes the state has cast over the years for Republican candidates for president is not taken into account, only whether the Republican candidate carried the state.

In contrast, the Democratic party focuses on a state's voting record in recent presidential elections, not gubernatorial, senatorial, or congressional ones; moreover, it is concerned with the total number of popular votes cast for its presidential candidates. A populous two-party state such as New York is advantaged by that system. Its size means that it will cast a large number of popular votes for the Democratic presidential candidate whether that person carries the state or not, and it does not matter that Democratic candidates lose nonpresidential elections. However, a small state in which the Democrats are dominant, such as Rhode Island, is disadvantaged. Even if recent Democratic presidential candidates carried the state, they did not win a large number of popular votes, and Democratic victories in nonpresidential elections earn the state no bonus votes.

Selecting Delegates

State delegates to the national conventions of both parties are chosen by one of three methods. The first is selection by *party leaders,* such as members of the state central committee, the party chairperson, or the governor (if the party controls that office). The second is choice by a *state convention* composed of persons themselves elected at caucuses and conventions held in smaller geographical areas, such as precincts, wards, counties, and congressional districts. The third is direct election by the voters themselves in *presidential primaries.* States often combine methods, using a primary to elect district delegates but allowing their state committees to choose "at-large" delegates (those representing the whole state).

Traditionally, persons active in party affairs, public and party officials referred to as "professionals," dominated the selection of delegates. This was only natural under the first method, in which party officials formally appoint the delegates. Professionals also dominated under the second system because they manipulated the caucuses and conventions into choosing themselves and their loyal supporters as delegates. Moreover, professionals ran successfully as delegates in presidential primaries, and because many states did not require them to vote at the national convention for the candidate favored by rank-and-file voters in the primary, delegates were free to vote their own presidential preferences instead.

Between 1968 and 1980, however, there was a definite trend away from control by party professionals and toward increased participation by rank-and-file voters. In 1968 only seventeen states chose delegates by a presidential primary; in 1980, thirty-one did. Meanwhile, the proportion of total national convention delegates chosen in primaries climbed from 38 percent to 72 percent. In the process, the primary replaced the state convention system as the dominant method for choosing delegates to the national convention.

Many of the new primary laws passed between 1968 and 1980 also increased the influence of rank-and-file voters over their party's ultimate choice for president. States encouraged delegates chosen in primaries to indicate which candidate they personally supported for president so that voters could predict how their delegates would vote at the national convention. Some states also permitted voters themselves to indicate their personal preference for president and legally bound the delegates to support the preferred candidates for one or more ballots at the convention. Moreover, under many of the new state laws, a presidential candidate's name was placed on the ballot if his or her candidacy was recognized by the national news media. A candidate who wanted to be removed from the race had to file an affidavit swearing that he or she was not a candidate in any state that presidential election year. This system prevented candidates from choosing which state primaries they would enter, thus allowing voters to pass judgment on a broader range of potential nominees than would otherwise have been available to them.

The trend toward greater influence for rank-and-file voters turned around between 1980 and 1984 as six jurisdictions abandoned the primary in favor of the caucus-convention for selecting delegates to the national convention. As a result, the proportion of delegates chosen by state presidential primaries declined from 72 percent to 54 percent.

By 1984 the system that emerged for choosing delegates to the national convention was thus a "mixed" one, with twenty-three states and the District of Columbia using primaries and twenty-seven states using caucus-conventions. As Figure 1-1 indicates, there were some regional variations in the use of the two methods: western states generally preferred caucus-conventions; northeastern states, primaries; and the midwestern and southern states were fairly evenly divided between the two methods.

In addition to the passage of laws by state legislatures, the national political parties themselves have taken action to reform the process for selecting delegates to the national conventions.

Democrats. The vast changes the Democratic party made in its procedures after 1968 can be traced to that year's convention in Chicago. It was an assembly marked by acrimonious debates within the convention hall over the Vietnam War and by bloody battles outside the convention arena between war protestors and the police. The 1968 delegates were concerned that much of the chaos of that convention occurred because the regular party organization was impervious to the will of rank-and-file Democrats. (Sen. Hubert Humphrey won the nomination without entering a single presidential primary, because party leaders favoring him dominated the delegations of the caucus-convention states.) The delegates consequently adopted a resolution requiring state parties to give "all Democrats a full, meaningful, and timely opportunity to participate"

Figure 1-1 Delegate Selection Methods by State and Region, 1984

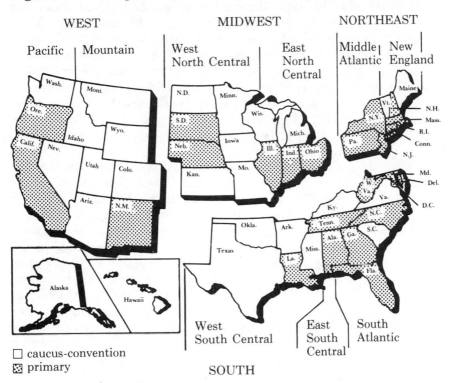

Source: *Congressional Quarterly Weekly Report,* June 2, 1984, 1317, and June 16, 1984, 1443.

in the selection of delegates. Not long after, the Democratic National Committee established a commission chaired by Senator McGovern of South Dakota to assist state parties in meeting that requirement. This action established a pattern: following the 1972 convention a new commission, this time under the leadership of Baltimore councilwoman Barbara Mikulski, continued the effort to change the delegate selection process. After the 1976 national convention, the party organized still a third commission, chaired by Morley Winograd (state chairperson of the Michigan Democratic party). In each case the commission recommended changes in rules affecting the selection of convention delegates for the next convention; most of these were adopted by the Democratic National Committee and ultimately by the Democratic national convention.

For the most part, the battle lines in this series of rules changes were drawn between party professionals and political "amateurs," persons not traditionally active in party affairs but who became involved because of an interest in a particular candidate or issue. The amateurs won the struggle to open up the selection process when the McGovern Commission recommended that states remove restrictive voter registration laws so that non-Democrats and unaffiliated voters could become party members. At the same time, the control of traditional party leaders over caucuses and conventions was reduced by regulations that forbade them to serve automatically as ex officio delegates and by requirements for written party rules, adequate public notice of meetings, and the elimination of proxy voting.

A second issue that plagued all three party commissions was the representation of particular groups within state delegations to the national convention. The amateurs scored an initial victory when the McGovern Commission recommended that minority groups, women, and young people (those aged eighteen to thirty) be represented in state delegations "in reasonable relationship to the groups' presence in the state." This recommendation led many states to adopt a quota system when they chose their delegates to the 1972 convention. Other minority groups, however, such as those of Italian and Polish descent, who had traditionally supported the party, questioned why they had not been included in the quotas. Other Democrats opposed the idea of quotas altogether because the quotas determined the results of the political process rather than merely the opportunity to participate in it—the traditional American concept of political equality. The Mikulski Commission did adopt the latter concept by eliminating the quotas in favor of more inclusive "affirmative action plans," whereby each state party undertook to encourage "minorities, Native Americans, women, and other traditionally underrepresented groups to participate and to be represented in the delegate selection process and all party affairs." The idea of quotas surfaced again, however, as professionals and amateurs battled over representation at the 1980 convention. This time each achieved a victory: the professionals won an increase in the size of state delegations by 10 percent to permit selection of state party and elected officials; the amateurs won the adoption of a rule requiring that state delegations comprise equal numbers of men and women.

A third major problem for all three party commissions was the division of state delegation votes among the various contending candidates. The McGovern Commission recommended that states abolish the "winner-take-all" primaries—whereby the candidate who received simply a plurality of the popular vote was awarded all the delegates—in favor of a provision for the "fair representation of minority views on presidential

14

candidates." California, however, refused to follow this recommendation (the commission only "urged" rather than "required" the action). At the 1972 convention, McGovern himself received all 271 votes of the California delegates, although he had beaten Humphrey in the primary by only 45 to 39 percent of the popular vote. The irony of that development led the Democrats to abolish statewide winner-take-all contests in 1976, so that candidates winning at least 15 percent of the votes in presidential primaries and caucus-convention meetings would receive their proportional share of a state's delegate votes. For the 1980 nomination, Democrats extended the proportional representation principle to district contests. The minimum cutoff figure for candidates entitled to delegate votes was determined by dividing the number of district delegates by 100. (In a district with five delegates, for example, the cutoff would be 20 percent.) In no case, however, was the cutoff figure to be higher than 25 percent, regardless of the number of delegates elected in a district.

The battle over rules for the selection of delegates to Democratic national conventions continued in the 1980s. The Democratic National Committee again appointed a commission—this one chaired by Governor James B. Hunt, Jr., of North Carolina—to develop rules for the 1984 nomination contest. This time party professionals were determined to establish rules that would give them a greater role in the nomination process and also facilitate the selection of "their" kind of candidate rather than an "outsider" like McGovern or Jimmy Carter. They clearly prevailed over the political amateurs in the changes proposed by the Hunt Commission and later adopted by the national committee and the 1984 convention. A bloc of "superdelegates" composed of party and elected officials (constituting some 14 percent of the convention votes) was created; state officials and Democratic members of the House and Senate were responsible for choosing these superdelegates (typically themselves), who were to go to the 1984 convention uncommitted. Another change also favored the states, particularly populous ones, by allowing them to use once again the winner-take-all principle in district contests and thereby reward a front-runner with a large bloc of delegate votes.[9] Finally, the new rules abolished a provision that bound all delegates to the 1980 national convention to vote on the first ballot for the candidate to whom they were linked in the state's delegate selection process. (The vital part this provision played in the 1980 convention will be discussed in Chapter 2.) The 1984 delegates were therefore legally free to vote as they desired at that year's convention.

Because unsuccessful Democratic candidates Gary Hart and Jesse Jackson were dissatisfied with the 1984 rules (which, they said, favored Walter Mondale), the national convention created the Fairness Commission to study their complaints and possibly reduce the role of party and elected officials in the 1988 nomination process. However, members of the new commission, chaired by Donald L. Fowler of South Carolina, followed the lead of Democratic national chairperson Paul G. Kirk, Jr., in developing rules they hope will build a consensus behind a candidate long before the 1988 national convention is held.

As a result, only minor changes will be made in the 1984 rules. In fact, the commission did not reduce but actually increased the number of super-delegates from about 550 to some 650, which means that all the Democratic governors, all the members of the Democratic National Committee, and 80 percent of the Democratic members of Congress will have delegate seats at the 1988 convention. The Fairness Commission also relaxed the 1984 rule that restricted participation in the nomination process to Democrats, so that states such as Wisconsin and Montana can conduct "open" primaries in 1988 with the approval of the national party. The only concession to the major critics of the 1984 rules was a change lowering the proportion of votes a candidate must receive in a primary or caucus to qualify for delegates from 20 to 15 percent. In early March 1986, the Democratic National Committee approved the recommendations of the Fairness Commission, which means that for the first time in a generation Democrats will be operating under essentially the same rules for two consecutive nomination contests.

Republicans. The Republican party also has made some changes in its delegate selection process even though its leaders did not face the pressures for reform that the Democratic leaders faced. A committee chaired by Rosemary Ginn, a Missouri member of the national committee, recommended proposals that were implemented in the choosing of delegates to the 1976 convention. Included were provisions, similar to those of the McGovern Commission, that reduced the influence of traditional party leaders by eliminating them as ex officio delegates, that regularized the nomination process by informing citizens how to participate in it, and that increased participation by opening the primaries and the state conventions to all qualified citizens.

At the same time, the Republican party has not attempted to regulate selection of national convention delegates nearly as extensively as has the Democratic party. The 1972 Republican national convention turned down recommendations of the Ginn Committee to include in future conventions persons under twenty-five years of age in "numerical equity to their voting strength in a state" and to have one man, one woman, one person under twenty-five, and one member of a minority group on each of the convention's principal committees. In 1975 the

Republican National Committee refused to adopt the recommendation of a new committee chaired by Rep. William Steiger of Wisconsin that all states be required to have their affirmative action plans approved by the national committee. Nor have the Republicans moved to abolish winner-take-all primaries, like the one in California. Thus the national Republican party has been much less willing than its Democratic counterpart to intervene in state decisions on the selection of delegates to the national convention.

Effect of Changes in Delegate Selection Rules

The rules changes made from 1968 to 1980 had a profound effect on the choosing of presidential nominees, particularly for the Democratic party. The proliferation of primaries and the deliberate lessening of the influence of party leaders in caucus-convention states made these leaders far less influential in the nomination process. Such professionals, who traditionally used their skills to select persons considered electable and loyal to the party (such as Humphrey), were largely replaced by political amateurs who supported "issue-oriented" and "antiestablishment" candidates for the presidency (such as McGovern and Carter).

Democratic rules designed to increase the representation of traditionally disadvantaged groups in the nomination process also brought the intended results. Women in particular benefited. In 1968, before the Democratic reforms, they constituted only 13 percent of the delegates at the Democratic convention. In 1972 that figure nearly tripled to 38 percent and, after a slight decline to 33 percent in 1976, rose to 50 percent in 1980 and 1984 as a consequence of the party's decision to require that both sexes be equally represented at the Democratic national convention.

Finally, rules changes ending the winner-take-all primary in favor of a proportional division of states' convention votes made victories in states such as California less important than they used to be. Although George McGovern owed his convention victory in 1972 to the 271 votes he won from that state, Jimmy Carter won his party's nomination both in 1976 and in 1980 without winning California. (Governor Jerry Brown carried the state in 1976; Kennedy carried it in 1980.) The proportional rule also encouraged candidates to participate in state primaries they did not expect to win, because they had a chance to receive some convention votes rather than being shut out completely, as had occurred in winner-take-all contests.

The 1984 rules favored by the party professionals also brought about the desired effects. Walter Mondale—the candidate they preferred—benefited by the new rules. He received an overwhelming share of the votes at the national convention from the superdelegates and did very well in states that used the winner-take-all principle in district contests to allocate delegates. He also won a greater number of votes in states that used caucuses to select their delegates than did Gary Hart or Jesse Jackson (recall that more states adopted this method in 1984). As a result, Mondale prevailed at the convention, even though his two rivals received a combined share of 55 percent of the votes cast in the primaries.

Financing Presidential Nomination Campaigns

Historically, restrictions on contributions to presidential campaigns have not worked. The federal government passed legislation in 1907 forbidding corporations to contribute money to presidential nominations and elections, but corporations easily circumvented the law by paying executives extra compensation, which they and their families subsequently contributed in their own, not the company, name. The 1947 Taft-Hartley Act prohibited contributions by labor unions, but unions, too, evaded the restrictions by forming political action committees (PACs) to solicit voluntary donations from members and to spend the funds in the committee's name. Finally, the Hatch Act of 1940 (which limited individual contributions to a federal candidate to $5,000) and a federal tax law that imposed progressive tax rates on contributions of more than $3,000 to a single committee both proved ineffective because numerous committees were formed for a single candidate, and each committee was entitled to accept a $5,000 contribution.

The move for campaign reform began with President John F. Kennedy, who was sensitive to the advantages wealth gave a candidate.[10] He appointed the Commission on Campaign Costs, which issued a report in 1962 proposing public reporting of campaign expenditures, tax incentives for contributors, and matching funds for presidential candidates. Nothing came of the proposals during the 1960s, but they laid the groundwork for the wave of reform that swept the country in the 1970s. In 1971 and again in 1974 Congress passed legislation affecting campaign financing. In January 1976, however, in *Buckley v. Valeo*,[11] the Supreme Court ruled certain provisions of the legislation unconstitutional; later that year Congress responded by enacting still further regulations governing the use of money in federal elections. Finally, in 1979 Congress added more amendments to the campaign finance legislation.

A variety of regulations therefore govern the financial conduct of presidential campaigns. The following sections discuss the major ones affecting the nomination process. (Some of the provisions also apply to the general election campaign, which is treated in Chapter 3.)

Disclosure of Information. Presidential candidates and committees are required to provide full information on the financing of their campaigns. They must report the names of all contributors who give $200 or more and itemize expenses of $200 or more. This information is filed with the Federal Election Commission (FEC), the agency responsible for administering the campaign legislation. The FEC is a bipartisan body of six members nominated by the president and confirmed by the Senate.

Limits on Contributions. Individuals are limited to contributions of $1,000 to a presidential candidate for each election (the nomination and general election are considered separate contests), $5,000 to a political action committee (one that contributes to more than one candidate), $20,000 to the national committee of a political party, and a total contribution of no more than $25,000 a year. Presidential candidates are free to spend an unlimited amount of their own money and their immediate family's money on their campaigns, but if they accept public financing, their contributions to their own campaign are limited to $50,000 per election.

Limits on Spending. Candidates may spend as much as they wish on presidential campaigns unless they accept public financing, in which case limitations apply. For the 1984 presidential campaign, limits for the nomination process included a national ceiling of $20.2 million plus 20 percent for fund-raising costs—a total of $24.4 million. In addition, each state imposes spending limitations based on its population. In 1984, California had the highest spending limit, $5.4 million; the lowest figure, which applied to a number of small states, was $404,000.

Independent Campaign Expenditures. There is no limitation on independent campaign expenditures, that is, those made by individuals or political committees advocating the defeat or election of a candidate but not made in conjunction with the candidate's campaign. However, individuals or committees making such expenditures in amounts of more than $250 must file a report with the FEC and must state, under penalty of perjury, that the expenditure was not made in collusion with the candidate.

Public Financing. Candidates for the presidential nomination who are able to raise $100,000 in individual contributions, with at least $5,000 collected in twenty different states, receive federal matching funds equal to the total amount of their contributions of $250 or less. (By checking a box on their federal income tax forms, taxpayers authorize the federal government to set aside $1.00 of their tax payments for public financing of campaigns.) In 1984, $10.1 million in federal matching funds was available to each candidate for the nomination process. The federal government also provided the Democratic and Republican parties up to $6 million to finance their nominating conventions.

Like the alteration in delegate selection rules, campaign finance legislation has had a significant effect on presidential nominations. The sources and techniques for raising funds have radically changed. Rather than depending upon a few "fat cats" to finance their campaigns (in 1968 insurance executive W. Clement Stone gave $2.8 million to Richard Nixon's campaign), candidates now raise funds from a large number of small individual contributors, primarily through direct mail solicitation.[12] Public funds also make it possible for persons who formerly could not afford to mount a nomination campaign to do so. Sen. Fred Harris had to abandon a presidential bid in 1972 because he could not raise money from large contributors; but with federal matching funds available, he was able to run in 1976. Moreover, even single-issue Right to Life candidate Ellen McCormack was able to qualify for federal funds that year. At the same time, the new method of raising funds from a large number of individuals and thereby qualifying for federal matching money means that candidates tend to start their campaigns earlier than they formerly did. Finally, as election specialist Herbert Alexander suggests, public funding also helps "free each candidate's personal organization from the party hierarchy."[13]

Thus a variety of rules help shape the nomination contest. The remainder of the chapter focuses on the people directly affected by such rules—the presidential candidates themselves.

The Pool of Candidates

Unlike the rules governing the nomination process, those relating to the qualifications of presidential candidates are minimal. To be eligible for the presidency, individuals need meet only three requirements, set forth in Article II, Section 1, of the Constitution. One must be a "natural born" citizen,[14] at least thirty-five years of age, and a resident of the United States for fourteen years or longer. In 1974, Austin Ranney estimated that some 80 million Americans met these constitutional requirements.[15] Today the figure would be even higher.

Although there are few *formal* requirements for the presidency, there are major *informal* ones. Persons who entertain presidential ambitions (the bug is considered to be virtually incurable once it strikes) must possess what is generally called "political availability"; that is, they must have the political experiences and personal characteristics that presumably make them attractive to political activists and to the general voting public as well. There is, however, no definite checklist of job qualifications for the presidency. The closest that one can come to determining what particular political experiences and personal characteristics put an individual in line for a presidential nomination is to look at past candidates. Even this approach poses some difficulties, since the attitudes of political leaders and the American public change over time. The following discussion, which focuses on the period since the election of Franklin D. Roosevelt in 1932, analyzes the informal standards of presidential availability that operated during that era, including how some of those standards have changed in the past half-century.

Political Experience of Presidential Candidates

Like their predecessors, most nominees and other major presidential candidates since 1932 (see Appendix C for a list of the Republican and Democratic aspirants) had previous service in a civilian, elective, political office. (The two exceptions were Wendell Willkie, who was president of a public utility company when he was nominated by the Republicans in 1940, and Dwight D. Eisenhower, a career military man and World War II hero, who became the successful GOP candidate in 1952.) Although many nominees and other major candidates occupied a variety of such political posts during the course of their political careers, the particular offices they held immediately before becoming presidential candidates were relatively limited. As the following discussion indicates, the sources of candidates for the party out of power are different from the ones that prevail for the party that occupies the presidency.

Since 1932 a principal recruiting ground for the party out of power—one long popular in U.S. politics—has been a *state governorship.* Throughout this era, both major parties looked to governors as promising candidates. Moreover, from 1932 through 1956 governors tended to become the nominees: Democrat Franklin Roosevelt of New York in 1932 and Republicans Alfred Landon of Kansas in 1936 and Thomas Dewey of New York in 1944. After a hiatus from 1960 through 1972, the state governorship once again emerged as the dominant background for successful presidential nominees of the party out of power when former Georgia governor Jimmy Carter won the Democratic presidential nomination in 1976 and when former California governor Ronald Reagan became the Republican standard-bearer in 1980.

The other major office from which presidential candidates of the party out of power have been recruited since 1932 is that of *U.S. senator.* Like governors, senators were major presidential candidates throughout that period. The particular era in which they tended to become the nominees was 1960 through 1972. During this period, the Democrats nominated senators John Kennedy of Massachusetts in 1960 and George McGovern of South Dakota in 1972, and the Republicans chose Barry Goldwater of Arizona in 1964.[16]

Several factors have increased the importance of the Senate as a recruiting ground for presidents. As Nelson Polsby points out, the nationalization of American politics has tended to shift political attention away from the state capitals to Washington, D.C., and senators have taken advantage of the opportunity to project themselves over the national news media concentrated there.[17] Also, senators increasingly have associated themselves with major public policies, a development that provides them great political visibility. Beyond this, the nation's greater involvement in foreign affairs since World War II naturally has placed the Senate in the public eye because of the influential role it plays in the conduct of relations with other countries. Moreover, the six-year term of senators enables them to try for the presidency without giving up their legislative seat: of the senators who have run for the presidency since 1922, only Barry Goldwater lost his place in the upper chamber as a result of his candidacy.[18]

In recent years governors seeking the presidency have faced several disadvantages. State chief executives no longer hold as crucial a position in the presidential selection process as they did when, as heads of state delegations, they negotiated at the national convention with their peers to choose the party's nominee (who frequently turned out to be a governor). Another handicap of recent governors who aspire to the presidency is that only those from states with large cities that serve as communications centers for the nation, such as New York, Los Angeles, and Chicago, receive as much publicity as national officials in Washington, D.C. In addition, governors have no responsibilities of consequence in foreign affairs and frequently do not appear well-versed in such matters. They also are more tied to their home states (particularly when the state legislature is in session) than are senators, who are expected to move freely about the country. Finally, many governors serve short stints in office—in some cases because of legal limitations on their tenure, in others because they fail to meet public expectations that they will solve major domestic problems without increasing taxes. They therefore find it difficult to become sufficiently well known to be viable presidential candidates.

Carter's election in 1976 and Reagan's bid for the nomination that year and election in 1980 indicate, however, that governors possess some advantages as candidates, particularly if they are *not* occupying that office at the time they seek the presidency. Both men were free to devote themselves full-time to the demanding task of winning the nomination, an opportunity not available to senators with heavy legislative duties who sought the presidency in both of those years (for example, Democrats Frank Church and Henry Jackson in 1976 and Republicans Howard Baker and Robert Dole in 1980). Both Carter and Reagan also benefited from the recent anti-Washington mood of the voters, which has made voters receptive to candidates who had not served in a national office. Citizen concern with the burgeoning costs of government and the problems of controlling the federal bureaucracy could continue to make governors attractive presidential candidates: they can claim valuable executive experience in managing large-scale public enterprises and thousands of state government employees in contrast to a senator's essentially legislative duties and small personal staff. Finally, the decline in the public's concern over foreign affairs compared with the domestic economy in recent years may counteract the advantages senators held over governors as presidential candidates before the end of the Vietnam War.

It is probable that the offices of both U.S. senator and state governor will continue to be major recruitment grounds for presidential candidates of the party out of power. At this writing (August 1987), three of the seven major Democratic candidates are sitting senators—Joseph Biden of Delaware, Albert Gore, Jr., of Tennessee, and Paul Simon of Illinois. The aspirants also include a sitting governor, Michael Dukakis of Massachusetts, and a former governor, Bruce Babbitt of Arizona. Also running are Rep. Richard A. Gephardt of Missouri and civil rights activist Jesse Jackson. (See Appendix B for the backgrounds of major candidates in the Republican and Democratic parties.)

For the party that occupies the presidency, *that office itself* is the major source of its candidates. In only three instances since 1932 has the incumbent chief executive not been his party's subsequent nominee: in 1960 when Republican Dwight Eisenhower was precluded from running again by the Twenty-second Amendment,[19] and in 1952 and 1968 when Democratic presidents Harry S Truman and Lyndon B. Johnson chose not to seek another term. The exact reasons for Truman's and Johnson's decisions are unknown, but both held office at the time of highly unpopular wars—those in Korea and in Vietnam. In addition, both had been challenged and embarrassed politically in the New Hampshire primary; Truman by Sen. Estes Kefauver of Tennessee and Johnson by Sen. Eugene McCarthy of Minnesota.

When the incumbent president decides not to run, recent experiences indicate that the office of *vice president* becomes a major source of presidential candidates for the party in power. In 1960 the Republicans chose Richard Nixon, virtually without opposition. (Governor Nelson Rockefeller of New York had considered making a bid that year but decided not to run when he determined early on that the vice president had the nomination locked up.) In 1968, the Democrats chose Vice President Hubert Humphrey as their nominee, but only after he had overcome the challenge of Senator McCarthy and after the assassination of Sen. Robert Kennedy of New York in early June ended Kennedy's candidacy. Only in 1952 was the incumbent vice president, Alben Barkley, denied the presidential nomination: at the time he was seventy-five years old and not considered to be a major figure in the party.[20] In that instance, the principal candidates came from the traditional training grounds already discussed: the party's nominee, Adlai Stevenson, was the governor of Illinois; contenders Estes Kefauver of Tennessee and Richard Russell of Georgia represented their states in the U.S. Senate.

Incumbent presidents have natural advantages when it comes to winning their party's nomination. It is difficult for a party to admit to the voters that it made a mistake four years before when it nominated the candidate who won the presidency. As discussed in the next chapter, incumbents also have several political weapons they can use against candidates who seek to deny them their party's nomination. As a result, even unpopular presidents tend to be renominated. The Republicans chose Herbert Hoover again in 1932 in the midst of the Great Depression; and the Democrats renominated Jimmy Carter in 1980 when both inflation and unemployment were high, Americans were being held hostage in Iran, and Soviet troops occupied Afghanistan. Moreover, even vice presidents who succeeded to the presidency on the death or resignation of their predecessors were nominated by their party in the period since 1932—Democrats Harry Truman and Lyndon Johnson and Republican Gerald R. Ford.

Recent developments also help explain why incumbent vice presidents are now more likely to win their party's nomination in their own right than they were in the past.[21] Presidential candidates of late are tending to choose more capable running mates, which makes these persons more viable prospects for the presidency itself. In addition, recent presidents are assigning their vice presidents more meaningful responsibilities than their predecessors did. These duties include participating in political party activities (especially campaigning in off-year elections), which helps them forge ties with party chieftains; serving as liaisons with social groups, which draws vice presidents to the attention of group leaders; and acting as emissaries to foreign countries, which makes them visible to the general public.

The Republican party faces an unusual situation in choosing the nominee for the 1988 election because of the large number of major candidates—six as of August 1987—in the race to succeed Ronald Reagan, the ineligible incumbent. The contenders come from a variety of political backgrounds—Vice President George Bush, Kansas senator Robert Dole, former Delaware governor Pierre (Pete) du Pont, New York representative Jack Kemp, former secretary of state Alexander Haig, and evangelist Marion G. (Pat) Robertson. (See the profiles of these candidates in Appendix B.)

Personal Characteristics of Presidential Candidates

Writing in 1959, journalist Sidney Hyman listed several "tests" of personal characteristics that had been applied to presidential nominees over the years.[22] It is instructive to consider whether these informal qualifications continued to apply in the seven presidential contests that have occurred since that time. Hyman has drawn the following conclusions:

- Preferred candidates come from states that have a large electoral vote and a two-party voting record.
- Candidates from big northern states are favored over those from southern states.
- Conventions nominate only persons who are, or who can be made to appear, hospitable to the many economic interests in the nation.
- Presidential candidates, like the English Crown, are expected to represent an idealized version of home and family life.
- Although the majority of Americans live in large urban centers, preferred candidates come from small towns.
- Preferred candidates come from English ethnic stock.
- Nominating conventions have created an extraconstitutional religious test by their decisive preference for Protestant hopefuls.

Although many of the candidates in presidential contests since 1960 satisfied the above tests, some clearly did not. Past geographical preferences for nominees from northern, two-party states with a large electoral vote failed to prevent the nomination of Barry Goldwater, from Arizona; Johnson, from Texas; Humphrey and Mondale, from Minnesota; McGovern, from South Dakota; or Carter, from Georgia. Nor were all the candidates from small towns. Nixon grew up on the outskirts of Los Angeles; John and Robert Kennedy, outside Boston. Goldwater spent his young adult years in Phoenix, Humphrey in Minneapolis, and Edmund (Jerry) Brown in Sacramento. Reagan was raised in a small town (Dixon,

Illinois), but his political career had its roots in the Los Angeles area of California.

Other of Hyman's tests pertaining to the social backgrounds of candidates also failed to apply to several candidates since 1960. John Kennedy's candidacy in 1960 violated the traditional preference for Protestants. Once he won, little was made of the fact that his brothers Robert and Edward were also Roman Catholic, as were other Democratic hopefuls—Eugene McCarthy and Edmund Brown (who even received training as a Jesuit priest). Nor did Republicans seem concerned that Senator Goldwater, though an Episcopalian, came from Jewish background on one side of the family. The related, traditional preference for English stock did little to deter the candidacies of the Kennedys, McCarthy, and Reagan of Irish background, Goldwater of Russian background, or Mondale of Norwegian background.

In addition, several presidential candidates since 1960 could not be said to represent an idealized version of home and family life. In 1963 Nelson Rockefeller divorced his wife of over thirty years and remarried a much younger woman, a divorcée whose previous husband won custody of the children of that marriage. In 1976 Democratic candidate Morris Udall was divorced, and in 1980 it was widely known that Edward Kennedy's marriage was in serious trouble (he and his wife subsequently separated). Edmund Brown was unmarried and at one time was reputed to be having an affair with rock singer Linda Ronstadt. Although none of these candidates won their party's nomination, Reagan, also divorced, was both nominated and elected in the 1980 contest and thereby became the country's first divorced president.

Finally, several recent presidential candidates failed to meet Hyman's 1959 test of being or appearing to be hospitable to the many economic interests in the nation. Goldwater had private business interests (his family owned a department store), and Nixon had close political ties to conservative California businessmen, as did Reagan, who, like Goldwater, also clearly embraced the tenets of private enterprise. Humphrey, Edward Kennedy, and Mondale were allied closely with organized labor; and McGovern was identified with economic underdogs, as indicated in the 1972 campaign by his espousing a $1,000 grant for all Americans.

Thus, none of Hyman's informal qualifications have stood the test of time. Changes in the nomination process itself as well as broader currents in U.S. society have altered many of the major considerations underlying the choice of presidential candidates.[23] The development of a more common culture and the nationalization of American life in general, brought about by improved means of communication and transportation, have reduced the importance of parochial concerns—the religious, ethnic, or geographical background of a candidate—and increased the emphasis on the experience presidential candidates have had in the national political arena and their association with national issues. Moreover, as other groups that are still socially or politically disadvantaged—blacks, women, immigrants from Mexico, eastern and southern Europe, and the Far East—begin to occupy governorships and seats in the U.S. Senate, from which U.S. chief executives traditionally have been recruited, they will increase their chances of becoming serious candidates for the presidency.[24]

Notes

1. Hugh Heclo, "Presidential and Prime Ministerial Selection" in *Perspectives on Presidential Selection,* ed. Donald R. Matthews (Washington, D.C.: Brookings, 1973), 25.
2. William Chambers, *Political Parties in a New Nation: The American Experience, 1776-1809* (New York: Oxford University Press, 1963), chap. 2.
3. In the early 1820s the Republican party became known as the Democratic-Republicans and in 1840 was officially designated as the Democratic party (Paul David, Ralph Goldman, and Richard Bain, *The Politics of National Party Conventions* [New York: Vintage, 1964], chap. 3).
4. Joseph Charles, *The Origins of the American Party System* (New York: Harper Torch, 1956), 83-94.
5. Gerald Pomper, *Nominating the President: The Politics of Convention Choice* (New York: Norton, 1966), 17.
6. David, Goldman, and Bain, *Politics of National Party Conventions,* 50.
7. The National Republican party was soon to give way to the Whigs, with many Whig supporters joining the Republican party when it was formed in the 1850s (ibid., 57-59).
8. Ibid., 61.
9. Some states used another variant in 1984, the "winner-take-more" principle, whereby the leading candidate in a district received a "bonus" delegate, and the remainder of the delegates were divided among the candidates in proportion to the votes they received.
10. Herbert E. Alexander, *Financing Politics: Money, Elections and Political Reform,* 2d ed. (Washington, D.C.: CQ Press, 1980), 27.
11. 424 U.S. 1 (1976).
12. Although political action committees can help finance nomination campaigns, their contributions are not matched by federal funds as are those of individuals.
13. Alexander, *Financing Politics,* 98.
14. Naturalized citizens (such as former secretary of state Henry Kissinger, who was born in Germany) do not meet this requirement. There is some question whether persons born abroad of American citizens (such as George Romney,

former governor of Michigan and 1968 presidential aspirant, who was born of American parents in France) are also legally barred from the presidency by this stipulation.

15. Austin Ranney, "Changing the Rules of the Nominating Game," in *Choosing the President,* ed. James David Barber (Englewood Cliffs, N.J.: Prentice-Hall, 1974), 71.
16. It should be noted that on occasion the party out of power draws on a third source for candidates—*defeated presidential candidates.* Since 1932, the Republicans have chosen Thomas Dewey and Richard Nixon, and the Democrats, Adlai Stevenson, to run for the presidency a second time. Only Nixon was successful.
17. Nelson Polsby, *Congress and the Presidency,* 3d ed. (Englewood Cliffs, N.J.: Prentice-Hall, 1976), 99-102.
18. William Keech and Donald Matthews, *The Party's Choice* (Washington, D.C.: Brookings, 1976), 23.
19. That same amendment will prevent Ronald Reagan from seeking the office again in 1988.
20. It should also be noted that a former vice president may ultimately become a presidential candidate: Walter Mondale served in that office from 1977 to 1981 and became the Democratic presidential candidate in 1984.
21. Before Richard Nixon's selection in 1960, the last incumbent vice president to be nominated was Martin Van Buren in 1836.
22. Sidney Hyman, "Nine Tests for the Presidential Hopeful," *New York Times,* January 4, 1959, sec. 5, 1-11.
23. With so many marriages now ending in divorce, it is not surprising that the American public has become more tolerant of presidential candidates who have had marital difficulties.
24. Jesse Jackson not only finished third behind Walter Mondale and Gary Hart for the 1984 Democratic nomination but as of July 1987 was the leading candidate for the 1988 nomination. At that same time, Rep. Patricia Schroeder of Colorado was also mentioned as a possible Democratic candidate in 1988.

Selected Readings

Alexander, Herbert E. *Financing Politics: Money, Elections, and Political Reform.* 3d ed. Washington, D.C.: CQ Press, 1984.

Crotty, William, and John S. Jackson III. *Presidential Primaries and Nominations.* Washington, D.C.: CQ Press, 1985.

Grassmuck, George, ed. *Before Nomination: Our Primary Problems.* Washington, D.C.: American Enterprise Institute, 1985.

Shafer, Byron E. *Quiet Revolution: The Struggle for the Democratic Party and the Shaping of Post-Reform Politics.* New York: Russell Sage Foundation, 1983.

The Nomination Campaign

2

The nomination campaign is a long, winnowing process in which each of the two major parties chooses from a large pool of potential candidates the one person who will represent the party in the general election. As political scientist Austin Ranney points out, the nomination phase is more important than the election stage of the campaign, because "the parties' nominating processes eliminate far more presidential possibilities than do the voters' electing processes." [1]

There are several important differences between the campaign for the nomination and the campaign preceding the general election. A nomination campaign is much less structured than a general election campaign. Rather than contending with one known opponent representing the other major political party, aspirants for their party's nomination typically do not know how many opponents they will face or who they will be. In contrast to the general election's relatively short, definite campaign period (from Labor Day in early September to election day in early November), the nomination campaign is long and indefinite, starting when candidates begin their quest for the presidency. Unlike the general election campaign, which occurs in all fifty states simultaneously, the nomination campaign takes place in stages. Finally, presidential nominees can use their party label to attract votes and can count on party leaders to work in their campaign, but candidates for their party's nomination must develop other types of political appeals to attract the support of the "selectorate" and a personal organization to work on their behalf.

The highly unstructured nature of the presidential nominating process causes great uncertainties for candidates in planning and conducting the campaign. A further complication is that most first-time candidates must organize a nationwide political campaign, a task that, by comparison, dwarfs the effort of winning a Senate seat or governorship in even the largest states. As the following discussion indicates, important decisions have to be made all along the road to the party's nomination.

Early Maneuvering

Although the formal nomination process does not start until the beginning of the election year (since 1976, with the Iowa caucuses), political maneuvering takes place long before that time. A few days after the 1972 presidential election, for example, Jimmy Carter's staff laid out a plan for winning the 1976 Democratic nomination. Shortly after vice-presidential candidate Walter Mondale lost the 1980 election, he began his quest for the 1984 Democratic presidential nomination.

Journalist Arthur Hadley calls this political interval between the election of one president and the first primary before the next presidential election "the invisible primary." [2] By this he means that a political contest occurs during this time that has many of the characteristics of the actual state primaries. The major difference between the two types of primary is that the invisible one takes place behind the scenes as far as the general public is concerned, whereas American voters are very conscious of the regular primaries.

The invisible primary is a testing ground for the would-be president to determine whether his candidacy is viable. One factor that Hadley emphasizes is a psychological one: is the candidate willing to undergo the grueling process needed to win, characterized by extended absences from home, long hours on the campaign trail, and short, sometimes sleepless nights? Vice President Walter Mondale, an early casualty of the period preceding the 1976 election, withdrew from the race in November 1974 with the following statement: "I found I did not have the overwhelming desire to be President which is essential for the kind of campaign that is required. I don't think anyone should be President who is not willing to go through fire." [3]

An important task for the presidential candidate at this stage is the assembling of a staff to plan the campaign strategy and of what Hadley calls a "constituency," a larger group of workers who are willing to do the advance work necessary to organize states for the upcoming primary and caucus-convention contests. Recent Democratic party nominees benefited from having dedicated supporters who began their organizational activities very early. A full one and one-half years before the Wisconsin primary in April 1972, a young member of George McGovern's staff, Eugene Pokorny, began to build a base of operation there;[4] in early 1975 a Carter staffer, Tim Kraft, began putting together a Carter organization for the Iowa precinct caucuses to be held in January 1976;[5] and in 1979

Terry Turner was made director of Carter's field operations in Iowa for the 1980 election.

Perhaps the most important factor in this early phase is how would-be candidates fare with the media. As columnist Russell Baker notes, the members of the media are the "great mentioner," the source of name recognition and favorable publicity. Candidates who are ignored because reporters and commentators do not regard them as serious contenders find it almost impossible to emerge as viable presidential possibilities. Adverse comments can also seriously damage a candidacy: in his quest for the 1980 Democratic nomination, Edmund (Jerry) Brown was portrayed by the media as a "spacey," "far-out" politician whose ideas, rhetoric, and lifestyle disqualified him for the presidency. In that same contest, Edward Kennedy's 1979 interview with CBS commentator Roger Mudd turned out to be a disaster because the senator seemed unable to give an adequate explanation of his actions in the accidental drowning of a young woman, Mary Jo Kopechne, in 1969; of his strained relationship with his wife, Joan, and his alleged affairs with other women; and of why he wanted to be president and how his policies and political views differed from those of President Carter. Many observers concluded that the Massachusetts senator never recovered from that interview, which occurred before his official presidential campaign even began.

In contrast, candidates who tend to do well in the invisible primary exploit the advantages provided by the media. Early in his 1976 campaign Carter's staff recommended that he cultivate important political columnists and editors—such as *New York Times* columnist Tom Wicker and *Washington Post* chairman Katharine Graham—by making favorable comments on their articles and columns and, if possible, by scheduling visits with them. Some candidates enhance their presence in the print media through magazine articles or books published either earlier in their careers or during the nomination campaign itself; examples include John F. Kennedy's *Profiles in Courage*, Richard Nixon's *Six Crises*, and Jimmy Carter's *Why Not The Best?* They also use television and radio, appearing regularly on shows such as "Meet the Press." They may even use a syndicated radio program or news column of their own, as Ronald Reagan did to advance his political views and, indirectly, his candidacy.

People with presidential ambitions typically take additional steps to enhance their prospects with leaders of their party as well as with the public. In anticipation of the 1972 election, Edmund Muskie, Hubert Humphrey's running mate in 1968, began accepting speaking engagements outside his home state of Maine soon after he and Humphrey were defeated. Looking toward the 1976 election, Jimmy Carter assumed the position of coordinator of the 1974 Democratic congressional campaign, a job that took him to thirty states, where he had the opportunity to get acquainted with Democratic leaders. A trip abroad may also keep candidates in the news and, if they have not had much experience in foreign affairs, help to counteract the charge that they are not knowledgeable in this vital area that consumes so much of the U.S. president's time.

Another key aspect of the invisible primary is the raising of funds necessary for the nomination campaign. As previously explained, the new finance legislation, which favors raising money in small amounts from many individuals, requires candidates to get an early start in soliciting funds. In fact, financial maneuvering may precede the candidate's own personal campaign. In January 1977, with $1 million he had left over from his 1976 campaign, Ronald Reagan established a political action committee (PAC) called the Citizens for the Republic. In 1978 the organization contributed more than $600,000 to four hundred Republican candidates in federal, state, and local elections, but the remainder of its total expenditure of $4.5 million went to pay operating expenses and traveling costs for Reagan, who served as the principal speaker at political gatherings for the GOP candidates. Thus Reagan himself was the major beneficiary of the Citizens for the Republic: he ingratiated himself with the Republican candidates who received contributions from the organization and gained valuable contacts with Republican party supporters as well as the list of political contributors to the Citizens for the Republic, who were natural targets for his own fund raising for the 1980 presidential campaign. Walter Mondale established a PAC, Committee for the Future of America, that raised $24 million and contributed to more than two hundred House, Senate, and gubernatorial candidates in 1982.

As the presidential election year approaches, campaign fund raising moves into high gear. During the last three months of 1979, seven candidates each raised more than $1 million: Republicans John Connally, Reagan, George Bush, and Robert Dole and Democrats Kennedy, Carter, and Brown. Ultimately, six of the seven received federal matching funds (Connally chose to finance his campaign from private sources alone), as did Republican candidates John Anderson, Howard Baker, and Philip Crane, and Democratic long shot Lyndon LaRouche. Financing for the 1984 contest got off to an even earlier start: during the first three months of 1983, Mondale raised more than $2 million; Reubin Askew, $800,000; Gary Hart, $465,000; Alan Cranston, $440,000; and Ernest Hollings, almost $250,000.

In recent years presidential candidates have also found it wise to enter prenomination "popularity" contests held in some states, even though such contests have no legal effect on the composition of the state delegation to the national convention. The Carter forces packed a

Jefferson-Jackson Day fund-raising dinner held in Iowa in October 1975 and, consequently, won the straw poll taken there. Four years later members of Carter's staff worked hard to get his supporters elected as delegates to the Florida Democratic state convention held in November 1979; as a result, he clearly defeated Senator Kennedy in a straw vote taken at the convention. At the same time, Ronald Reagan was scoring a triumph over his Republican opponents in a comparable poll taken at the Republican state convention in Florida. Such popularity contests started earlier for the 1984 race: in January 1983, native son Cranston won a preferential poll at a Democratic party state convention in California; in April of that year, Mondale came out first in a similar poll conducted at a party convention in Kennedy's home state of Massachusetts. The following June, Cranston also scored victories in straw polls in Wisconsin and Alabama, and in October Mondale won in Maine.

The early phase of the 1984 contest took on a new dimension when both the AFL-CIO (American Federation of Labor and Congress of Industrial Organizations), with its 14 million members and 98 affiliated unions, and the National Education Association (NEA), the nation's largest individual labor union with 1.7 million members, endorsed Mondale as the Democratic candidate before the official state contests. Shortly thereafter, the National Organization of Women endorsed Mondale as well.

Although it appeared in mid-1987 that straw polls and interest group endorsements would be less prevalent in the 1988 nomination contest, particularly for Democrats, other developments emerged early in that race. Reporters from the *Miami-Herald* published a story about an alleged extramarital affair of the Democratic front-runner, Gary Hart; shorty thereafter he dropped out of the contest, thereby radically changing the nature of that race. Long-shot Bruce Babbitt, the former Arizona governor, began television advertising in Iowa far earlier than usual, hoping to create curiosity about his candidacy among party activists who would dominate the precinct caucuses there. He also engaged in an interparty debate with Republican candidate Pierre (Pete) du Pont, who, like Babbitt, was given little chance of winning his party's nomination. Two, more prominent candidates, Richard A. Gephardt (D-Mo.) and Jack F. Kemp (R-N.Y.), also participated in an interparty debate. All seven Democratic candidates appeared in a televised debate on William F. Buckley's program, "Firing Line."

The early phase of the nomination campaign, which political scientist Donald Matthews refers to as "the emergence of presidential possibilities," serves as a testing period for would-be candidates, especially those in the party out of office.[6] (For the party in power, the incumbent president is typically the front-running candidate to succeed himself.) Some drop out before the official campaign begins, as did Democratic senator Walter Mondale in 1975, Republican senator Lowell Weicker in 1979, and former Democratic senator Gary Hart in 1987. Others establish themselves as leaders in the public opinion polls taken at the beginning of the year and go on to win their party's nomination. As Table 2-1 shows, this was the prevailing pattern from 1936 through 1968. In two recent instances, however, the front-runner was ultimately replaced by a dark horse—McGovern, who was preferred by only 3 percent of the Democrats in January 1972, and Carter, the choice of only 4 percent in January 1976. Leaders in the polls therefore cannot afford to relax after achieving early popularity: the final choice of the nominee depends on presidential primaries as well as on caucus-convention contests.

Targeting the Nomination Campaign

Developments since 1968 have increased the number of state contests in which candidates participate. Primary laws in some states automatically place nationally recognized candidates on the ballot, thus forcing them to participate in contests they may prefer to bypass. The proportional representation feature of the national Democratic party rules and similar provisions in some Republican state contests encourage candidates to enter races they do not expect to win, because they receive some delegate votes even when they lose. Moreover, the selectorate expects candidates to show that they have political support in all parts of the country. As a result, in 1980 both Jimmy Carter and Edward Kennedy were on the ballot in thirty-four of the thirty-five Democratic preference primaries (ignoring only Michigan, where the primary results were not binding, and delegates were chosen in separate caucuses). Republican George Bush entered all thirty-four of the GOP preference primaries, and Ronald Reagan entered thirty-two (he was not on the ballot in Puerto Rico and the District of Columbia). In 1984, Mondale and Hart entered all twenty-five primaries, and Jesse Jackson, twenty-four (he was not on the ballot in Puerto Rico).

A candidate's name may appear on a state ballot, but that does not mean he or she will wage an all-out campaign in that state. Limitations of time and energy prevent active campaigning in every state. The allocation of money also becomes a major problem. Not only is there an overall restriction on spending (a total of $24.4 million in 1984 for those accepting public financing), but spending limits also apply in each state.

Table 2-1 Leading Presidential Candidates and Nominees, 1936-1984

Year	Leading candidate at beginning of election year [a]	Nominee
Party in power		
1936 (D)	Roosevelt	Roosevelt
1940 (D)	Roosevelt	Roosevelt
1944 (D)	Roosevelt	Roosevelt
1948 (D)	Truman	Truman
1952 (D)	Truman	Stevenson
1956 (R)	Eisenhower	Eisenhower
1960 (R)	Nixon	Nixon
1964 (D)	Johnson	Johnson
1968 (D)	Johnson	Humphrey
1972 (R)	Nixon	Nixon
1976 (R)	Ford [b]	Ford
1980 (D)	Carter [c]	Carter
1984 (R)	Reagan [d]	Reagan
Party out of power		
1936 (R)	Landon	Landon
1940 (R)	—	Willkie
1944 (R)	Dewey	Dewey
1948 (R)	Dewey-Taft	Dewey
1952 (R)	Eisenhower-Taft	Eisenhower
1956 (D)	Stevenson	Stevenson
1960 (D)	Kennedy	Kennedy
1964 (R)	—	Goldwater
1968 (R)	Nixon	Nixon
1972 (D)	Muskie	McGovern
1976 (D)	Humphrey [b]	Carter
1980 (R)	— [c]	Reagan
1984 (D)	Mondale [d]	Mondale

Source: Donald Matthews, "Presidential Nominations: Process and Outcomes," in *Choosing the President*, ed. James David Barber (Englewood Cliffs, N.J.: Prentice-Hall, 1974), 54.

[a] Dash (—) indicates that no single candidate led in the polls.

[b] The 1976 information was taken from the January Gallup poll.

[c] Carter led Kennedy in all Gallup polls conducted after the seizure of the hostages by Iran in November 1979. In a February 1980 Gallup poll listing eight candidates, 34 percent of Republican voters named Reagan as their first choice and 32 percent chose Ford; however, when the choice was narrowed to those two candidates, 56 percent preferred Ford and 40 percent, Reagan.

[d] Since President Reagan was unopposed for the Republican nomination, no preference poll was taken. A Gallup poll in mid-February 1984 showed, however, that 86 percent of Republicans approved the president's performance in office. The Gallup poll indicating Mondale to be the leading candidate among Democrats was taken in mid-November 1983.

Such considerations require presidential candidates to establish priorities among the large number of primaries and caucus-convention contests. The primaries, in particular, are important, because they determine more than half of the delegates to the national conventions. Moreover, candidates are much more likely to campaign personally and spend more money in states that hold primaries than in those that have caucus-conventions.[7]

Candidates take several factors into account when deciding which primaries they should emphasize in their nomination campaigns. One is the date of the primary. The earliest contest, traditionally New Hampshire, usually attracts most of the major contenders because it is the first test of popular sentiment of rank-and-file voters. Although the number of New Hampshire delegates is small (in 1984, 22 of 3,933 Democratic delegates, and 22 of 2,235 Republicans), it focuses immediate attention on the winner, as it did on John Kennedy in 1960 and Carter in 1976. Even if a candidate loses in New Hampshire but draws a greater percentage of the vote than expected, the media may interpret the results as a "moral" victory, a judgment that benefited Eugene McCarthy in 1968 and George McGovern in 1972. (It should be pointed out, however, that the media generally have not followed that practice in more recent nomination contests.)

New Hampshire appeals to presidential candidates for another reason: its small area and population make campaigning there manageable. Only about 20,000 Democrats were registered in 1976, and the Carter organization stated that it contacted about 95 percent of them.[8] The state was therefore ideal for the former governor in the early stages of the nomination contest: he had not yet acquired substantial financial resources for media expenditures, and his contingent of Georgia volunteers could conduct an effective door-to-door campaign.

Other primaries provide a late indication of voter preference. The California primary, for example, traditionally occurs near the end of the primary season. If the earlier primaries have not produced a clear favorite, the Golden State can determine who the party's nominee will be. Both Goldwater in 1964 and McGovern in 1972 owed their ultimate selection to their primary victories in California, which projected them as "winners" shortly before delegates throughout the country went to the national convention. The rules of the nomination contest also make California an attractive target for presidential candidates. It has the largest number of state delegates at each of the party conventions and, for Republicans, a winner-take-all provision that delivers those delegates in a solid bloc to the winner of the primary.

Other considerations besides timing and delegate strength affect candidates' decisions about where to concentrate campaign efforts. Naturally, they try to choose states where they think they have the best chance of winning. In 1976 and again in 1980 the Carter forces concentrated major efforts in his native South. In 1976 Henry Jackson chose Massachusetts and New York as special targets because both states contained many Catholics, Jews, and labor union members with whom the Washington senator felt he had close political ties. In 1984 Walter Mondale selected Pennsylvania and Illinois for the same reasons. Morris Udall in 1976, John Anderson in 1980, and Gary Hart in 1984 focused on Massachusetts and Wisconsin because they expected to do well in the liberal academic communities concentrated in those states. The two Republican contenders in 1976, Gerald R. Ford and Ronald Reagan, worked hard in their home states of Michigan and California to advance their candidacies, as did 1980 Democratic candidates Jimmy Carter in Georgia and Edward Kennedy in Massachusetts.

At times, however, candidates may deliberately choose to contest primaries that are not considered advantageous to them to demonstrate that they have a broader appeal than is generally recognized. John Kennedy went into the West Virginia primary in 1960 to prove that a Catholic could win in a state in which the population was 95 percent Protestant. In 1976 Jimmy Carter chose the Pennsylvania primary to show that a southern Baptist could do well in a northern industrial state with a large Catholic population. Both risks proved to be good ones that greatly advanced the Kennedy and Carter candidacies.

A major problem for candidates is properly managing a primary they clearly expect to lose. Many contenders have found that the most successful approach is to convince the public and particularly the media that they are not contesting the primary, so that a loss is not considered a genuine defeat. George McGovern successfully pursued that ploy in the Florida primary in 1972, as did Ronald Reagan in Wisconsin in 1976. This strategy also enables candidates to save their resources for more promising primaries.

Most important, candidates must avoid raising false expectations during the nomination campaign. In 1976, shortly before the New Hampshire primary, the Reagan staff released the results of a public opinion poll showing him to be ahead of Ford. When the California governor lost that primary by a single percentage point, the media interpreted the results as a serious defeat for him and a major victory for Ford. In 1980 John Connally decided to focus on the South Carolina primary as the one that would establish his candidacy; when he lost to Reagan there, the Texas governor was forced to withdraw from the race altogether.

Even though since 1972 primaries usually have been more consequential in nomination campaigns than caucus-convention contests, in some instances caucus-conventions become crucial. Since 1976 the Iowa caucuses have taken on major importance because they are the first test of the candidates' political strength, and the media therefore attach great significance to an Iowa victory.[9] In 1976 Jimmy Carter's successful campaign in Iowa established him as the Democratic pack leader; in 1980 his victory over Senator Kennedy in that state gave him a psychological edge in the New Hampshire primary a month later.

Caucus-convention states also become important if no clear victor emerges in the presidential primaries. In 1976 both Gerald Ford and Ronald Reagan diligently pursued delegates chosen in Republican party caucuses and conventions, especially in the period immediately preceding the Republican convention. In the end, Ford owed his nomination to the previously uncommitted delegations, such as Mississippi, that cast their ballots at the national convention in his favor.

Manipulating Political Appeals

No candidate in the nomination campaign has the option of using the party label against opponents in the same way he or she can in the general election. However, a president seeking renomination and facing possible challenges can emphasize that he is currently the representative of his party. He can suggest that persons who challenge him for the nomination are casting doubts on the good judgment of the party, which nominated him four years previously, and that a challenge would divide the party in the upcoming general election. The president can even intimate that attacks on him are in effect attacks on the country itself. President Carter and his spokespersons employed all these tactics in his 1980 contest with his major opponent, Senator Kennedy.

In contrast, the challenger of an incumbent president must make the challenge appear legitimate. Several ways are possible. One is to suggest that the incumbent president is not providing the leadership the nation requires. Another is to intimate that the president is such a weak candidate that he will take the party and its congressional, state, and local candidates down to defeat in November. A third is to avow that the president has not kept the promises he made in his previous campaign and that he has strayed from the traditional policies of his party. Senator Kennedy used all these appeals in his unsuccessful attempt to wrest the 1980 Democratic nomination from President Carter.

In a nomination campaign, the incumbent president also can use the powers of his office to great advantage. In a speech early in the 1980 campaign Senator Kennedy charged that the Carter administration's offer of $7 million to relieve starvation in Cambodia was woefully inadequate; two hours later the president called in television camera crews to announce that $69 million would be given to combat famine and to resettle Cambodian refugees in Thailand. The president also invited Democratic leaders to the White House, and their acceptance was considered an endorsement of Carter's renomination. Aware of Carter's power to approve or disapprove federal grants to states and cities, almost five hundred mayors, governors, and members of Congress attended these meetings to demonstrate their support for his candidacy. As the campaign progressed, the president continued to use the prerogatives of his office. The Sunday before the Iowa caucuses, he appeared on "Meet the Press" and announced that he would insist that U.S. athletes boycott the summer Olympics unless the Soviet Union withdrew its troops from Afghanistan. On the eve of the New Hampshire primary the president invited the U.S. Olympic hockey team to the White House for a televised congratulatory ceremony for its victory over the Soviet team. On the morning of the Wisconsin and Kansas primaries, Carter made a public announcement of a "positive step" toward the release of the hostages in Iran.

The incumbent president therefore has a clear advantage in a nomination campaign. He not only can invoke the symbol of party unity; he can also manipulate events to benefit his candidacy. Incumbency is particularly advantageous if foreign crises occur during the campaign period, for Americans tend to "rally 'round the flag," and hence their president, as they initially did in 1980 for Carter when Americans were taken hostage in Iran. A review of U.S. history clearly shows the superior campaign position of the incumbent: Franklin Pierce was the last president who actively sought his party's renomination and failed to obtain it when James Buchanan won the Democratic nomination from him in 1856.

Presidential candidates in the party out of power face an entirely different campaign situation. Although none of them has the problem of how legitimately to challenge an incumbent president, they do experience other difficulties. Typically, many candidates vie for their party's nomination, and each aspirant must find a way to distinguish himself from his opponents. (Table 2-2 presents information on the range of persons who sought or were considered to be principal candidates for the 1984 Democratic nomination.) A further complication is that the range of political views of the selectorate in the nomination campaign is narrower than that of the electorate in the general election: most Republicans participating in the nomination process are conservative; most Democrats, liberal.

Table 2-2 Major Candidates for 1984 Democratic Nomination

Candidate	Background	Political views[a]	Assets	Liabilities
Reubin Askew	Lawyer, former governor of Florida, born Sept. 11, 1928	Most conservative Democratic candidate; generally opposes abortion and domestic-content legislation	Moderate southerner	Not well known in national politics
Alan Cranston	Journalist, senator from California, born June 19, 1914	Very liberal; emphasizes nuclear freeze and domestic-content legislation; highly critical of "Reaganomics"	First Democratic candidate publicly to announce for the presidency; did well in early straw polls in California, Wisconsin, and Alabama	Oldest Democratic candidate and regarded as too liberal by some Democrats
John Glenn	Astronaut, senator from Ohio, born July 18, 1921	"Centrist" candidate; emphasizes values and morality rather than specific issues	Well known as senator because of his astronaut fame; was considered by many to have the best chance of defeating President Reagan	Started quest for presidency late, poor organization, not a good speaker
Gary Hart	Lawyer, senator from Colorado, born Nov. 28, 1936	Emphasizes "new" ideas and approaches to society's problems; critical of excessive expenditures on expensive weapons systems, favors arms control and a mutually verifiable nuclear freeze	Experience as campaign manager of George McGovern in 1972; appeals to young people, many independents, some Republicans	Seen by some as a "loner" in the Senate; did not do well in early state straw polls or in public opinion polls

Jesse Jackson	Minister, civil rights activist, born Oct. 8, 1941	Very liberal on economic and social issues; highly critical of U.S. policy in the Middle East as favoring Israel over Arab nations	Best speaker among Democratic candidates; has great appeal to young blacks	Lack of experience in public office; considered too radical by many moderate Democrats
Ernest Hollings	Lawyer, senator from South Carolina, born Jan. 1, 1922	No clear pattern to his political views; a hawk on national defense but opposes MX missile and B-1 bomber; favors government programs on food stamps and school lunches but opposes those for urban transit and urban redevelopment	Moderate southern candidate who proposed alternative to President Reagan's 1983 budget	Not well known nationally and disadvantaged by southern association with Jimmy Carter
George McGovern	Professor, former senator from South Dakota, 1972 Democratic presidential nominee, born July 19, 1922	Very liberal on economic and social issues; opposes U.S. intervention in Central America	Experienced in presidential campaigns and popular among liberals	Associated with major Democratic defeat in 1972 and late entry into race
Walter Mondale	Lawyer, former senator and vice president, born Jan. 5, 1928	Political protégé of Hubert Humphrey; very liberal on both economic and social issues; favors domestic content legislation and a nuclear freeze	Best organized and financed democratic candidate, favored by organized labor	Not dynamic speaker, poor on television, not favored generally by younger voters and independents

a Refers to views compared with other Democrats, not the general population.

The limited range of the selectorate's views creates problems for those who try to advance their candidacy by taking stands on the issues. A candidate who departs from the standard positions runs the risk of alienating a large number of party members; yet one who does not do so remains indistinguishable from the other candidates. Thus it was difficult for Democratic voters in 1984 to differentiate among the policy positions of liberal candidates Mondale, Cranston, and McGovern. The same was true in 1980 for Republicans attempting to distinguish among the political views of conservative candidates Reagan, Crane, Dole, and Connally. In contrast, Republican representative John Anderson in 1980 took policy positions very different from those of conservative Republicans. (He favored, for example, gun control, the Equal Rights Amendment, the imposition of an import fee on gasoline to discourage consumption, and the public funding of abortions.) As a result, he alienated many Republican voters and had to drop out of the Republican race and run as an independent candidate.

Denied the use of a party label, and facing the problems associated with taking stands on issues, candidates develop other types of political appeals in nomination campaigns. Most important is the projection of a personal image that reflects their most attractive attributes. In 1980 Senator Kennedy, for example, pictured himself as a strong leader who could handle the nation's mounting economic and foreign policy problems. Four years earlier Jimmy Carter sought to take advantage of the nation's distrust of public officials after the Vietnam War and Watergate by creating the image of an honest person and promising to make the government as "truthful, capable, and filled with love as the American people." Thus candidates seek to link their personal characteristics with the perceived needs of the times.

Another important technique used in nomination campaigns is to project oneself as a "winner." This appeal usually is adopted by candidates who do well in the early nomination contests. Confident after his victory over Reagan in the 1980 Iowa caucuses, Bush suddenly announced that his campaign had momentum, or what he referred to as "Big Mo." Unfortunately for Bush, Big Mo lasted only until the New Hampshire primary, which Reagan clearly won. Similarly, in the 1984 Democratic contest Walter Mondale asserted his invincibility after his decisive victory in Iowa; one week later, however, he was upset by Gary Hart in New Hampshire.

Presidential nomination campaigns, therefore, are characterized more by the manipulation of personal images and claims of winner status than by a discussion of the issues. Contributing greatly to this situation is the influence of the media in the nomination process.

Communicating Political Appeals

In 1984, 18 million voters participated in the Democratic primaries. The need to communicate with this vast number of people means that candidates must turn to the mass media. During the 1980 campaign the major candidates depended mainly on short television commercials to carry their messages. Jimmy Carter's advertisements stressed his character: one showed the president with his family and concluded with the statement, "Husband, Father, President. He's done these three jobs with distinction." Edward Kennedy's commercials carried a leadership theme: they focused on the senator looking forceful in Senate hearings and walking through enthusiastic crowds. In 1984, advertisements took a more negative tone: one for Mondale showed a blinking red telephone on the president's desk, raising the fear that Hart could not be entrusted with the "most awesome, powerful responsibility in the world." Hart countered with a political commercial that showed a burning fuse, as a voice suggested that Mondale would risk another Vietnam in Central America by leaving U.S. troops there and by "using our sons as bargaining chips."

Candidate debates became important in the 1980 GOP nomination contest. Reagan refused to participate in the initial, nationally televised one held in Iowa on the grounds that such verbal encounters would destroy party unity; George Bush did well in the debate (he quoted Yogi Berra's classic remark in alleging that Carter had made the "wrong mistake" in imposing an embargo on grain shipments to the Soviet Union), and went on to win the caucuses there. Reagan then switched tactics and engaged in two debates in New Hampshire. In the second one, originally scheduled to include only Reagan and Bush, the California governor outmaneuvered his opponent by suggesting that the debate be opened to other candidates; when Bush insisted on sticking to the terms of the original two-person encounter, he came across as selfish to the other Republican contenders and to many voters as well. Reagan won the New Hampshire primary and also prevailed in Illinois, where he did well in a multicandidate debate, which included Illinoisan John Anderson.

The Democratic candidates held about a dozen debates in 1984, but none was as crucial as the Reagan-Bush New Hampshire debate of 1980. One problem, particularly early in the nomination campaign, was the large number of candidates (eight in the debate before the Iowa caucus); it was difficult for viewers to keep straight which candidate said what. Nonetheless, these verbal encounters, called "media events" [10] by one scholar, did enable the candidates to confront one another with interesting questions. In Iowa, Hart asked Mondale to indicate a single, major domestic issue on which he disagreed with the AFL-CIO; in Atlanta, Mondale challenged Hart to spell out the substance of his "new ideas," making his point by using the famous line from the Wendy's commercial, "Where's the beef?"

More important, however, than candidate commercials or debates in campaign communications is the coverage of the nomination process by representatives of the media. Particularly influential are nationally syndicated newspaper columnists, such as David Broder, Jack Germond, and Jules Witcover; many people, including writers for local newspapers, take their cues about the candidates and the nomination contest itself from these media "heavies." (One observer refers to this tendency as "pack journalism." [11]) Principal network newscasters, such as Dan Rather, Peter Jennings, and Tom Brokaw, also have played an important role in recent nomination campaigns, since television evening news is the main source of political information for most voters.

As political scientist Thomas Patterson maintains, the mass media focus primarily on the presidential "game"—who is winning and losing, campaign strategy and logistics, and appearances and "hoopla." [12] Thus the chances of the contestants are calculated and their candidacies assessed by the extent to which they surpass or fall short of the media's predictions. The media also attempt to analyze the strategies of the candidates and how successful they are likely to be. Television in particular concentrates its attention on candidate appearances and crowd reactions to such appearances, as it tries to convey the visually exciting aspects of the campaign. [13] Patterson contends that the media devote far less coverage to what he calls the "substance" of the campaign— discussion of issues and policies, the traits and records of the candidates, and endorsements by political leaders.

The media downplay political issues and policies in nomination campaigns for several reasons. As previously discussed, it is difficult to focus effectively on issues when a number of candidates in a nomination contest hold very similar views. Moreover, today's nomination campaigns are so long that candidates' speeches become, from the media's point of view, "unnewsworthy," as the contenders repeat their stands on the issues again and again. Finally, many media representatives assume that most voters are not interested in the issues; in any event, it is difficult to present issues in depth—especially on television, where the average evening news story lasts only a little longer than one minute.

Patterson points out that the media are, however, interested in two kinds of issues. [14] One is the "clear-cut" issue, in which candidates take diametrically opposed stands on a matter of public policy. This opposition creates controversy, on which the media thrive. The other is "campaign" issues, those that involve errors of judgment by candidates, such as Jimmy Carter's remark in 1976 about the desirability of preserving the "ethnic purity" of city neighborhoods. A graphic illustration of the media's preoccupation with campaign issues rather than policy issues is Roger Mudd's previously mentioned interview with Edward Kennedy: it concentrated primarily on Mary Jo Kopechne's death at Chappaquiddick and barely touched on Kennedy's voting record on issues in his seventeen years in the Senate.

The media also devote little attention to how candidates have done in prior public offices. Before the state caucuses and primaries begin, commentators give some coverage to the candidates' records, but that interest declines when the presidential "game" begins. Only when a hiatus occurs in the primary campaign do the media generally return to an examination of the record. In April 1980, for example, during the three weeks between the Wisconsin and the Pennsylvania primaries, the media suddenly began producing detailed comparisons of Reagan's campaign statements and his actual performance as the governor of California.

Thus the media shape the nature of the nomination campaign. They tend to focus attention on the game aspects of the early contests, particularly those in Iowa and New Hampshire. According to Patterson, they typically employ a winner-take-all principle that gives virtually all the publicity, regardless of how narrow the victory or the number of popular votes involved, to the victorious candidate in a state contest. In the 1976 Iowa caucuses Carter's winning of about 14,000 voters, 28 percent of the 50,000 cast (he actually trailed the "uncommitted" group), was interpreted by Roger Mudd as making the Georgia governor a "clear winner" and as opening the "ground between himself and the rest of the so-called pack." [15] At times, however, the media may provide greater coverage to the runner-up: after winning a mere 16 percent of the votes in the Iowa caucuses in 1984, Hart received as much publicity as Mondale, who captured three times as many votes.[16]

Campaign Organization and Workers

Although the mass media play a major role in communicating political appeals to the selectorate, interpersonal contacts remain an important element in nomination campaigns. This is particularly true in states that use caucus-conventions to choose their delegates to the national convention. In those states people do not merely go into a voting booth to cast their ballots; rather, they must participate often in lengthy meetings and sometimes in confrontations with supporters of other candidates. A series of meetings usually takes place throughout the state political system until a state convention chooses the national convention delegates. Many people are unwilling to commit that much time and effort to the nomination process unless campaign workers contact them personally.

As the campaign progresses, a candidate must expand the previously mentioned "constituency" that developed in the early, prenomination stage of the process. In the past, candidates often turned to political professionals to sponsor and organize their campaign, as Hubert Humphrey did in 1968. The endorsement of party professionals, however, does not always ensure the nomination. In 1972, for example, the early endorsement of Sen. Edmund Muskie by a number of Democratic party and public officials did not prevent the party from ultimately choosing George McGovern, a candidate with whom many professionals were uncomfortable. In 1976, an "outsider," Jimmy Carter, won the Democratic nomination, even though he had virtually no initial support from his fellow governors or other members of the Democratic political establishment. Among Republicans, Sen. Barry Goldwater won the 1964 nomination despite the opposition of many party leaders and public officials.

Probably the only candidate today who is in a position to line up the support of party professionals is an incumbent president, for he can use his influence over the dispensation of federal grants as political leverage against his opponents. Even this weapon is not always successful, however. Mayor Jane Byrne of Chicago (successor to the most powerful political boss of recent times, Richard Daley) endorsed Senator Kennedy, not President Carter, in the 1980 Democratic contest. Moreover, even when an incumbent president does receive the political blessing of a key political figure, it may not be decisive: Carter lost the New York primary in 1980 to Kennedy even though the president was endorsed by Mayor Edward Koch of New York City.

Today's candidates generally build their personal organization from political amateurs who offer support because they agree with a candidate's stands on the issues or are attracted to his or her personality or political style. Amateurs constituted the base for the Goldwater movement in 1964, for Eugene McCarthy's "Children's Crusade" in 1968, for McGovern's "guerrilla army" in 1972, and for Reagan's conservative constituency in 1976 and again in 1980. Political scientist Jeane Kirkpatrick refers to such activists as a "new presidential elite." [17] Usually members of the upper middle class, such people have neither experience in nor loyalty to traditional party organizations. As Kirkpatrick contends, they typically take a keen interest in the intellectual and moral aspects of politics and use their verbal skills to great advantage in nomination politics.

At times, members of interest groups also endorse presidential candidates and furnish campaign workers for them. Some major labor unions participated actively in the 1980 Democratic contest. Edward Kennedy drew support from the International Association of Machinists and Aerospace Workers, and the National Education Association worked hard on President Carter's behalf. Both the AFL-CIO and the NEA endorsed Walter Mondale before the 1984 formal nomination process began and then played an important part in helping him secure the Democratic nomination.

Campaign Finance

Presidential candidates since the 1970s have started raising funds for their campaigns before the actual state contests begin. This solicitation of funds continues during the official campaign period itself. Candidates who do not do well in the first few primaries, however, tend to drop out of the race early on. One reason for their doing so is that, under the campaign finance law, federal matching funds must be cut off within thirty days if a candidate obtains less than 10 percent of the votes in two consecutive primaries. Even candidates who do not depend on matching funds may decide that a contest is hopeless; John Connally withdrew from the Republican race in early March 1980 after losing the South Carolina Republican primary to Reagan. (By that time the former Texas governor had spent $11 million of privately raised money and had won only one convention delegate.) Even candidates who score some successes in primaries may nonetheless develop financial problems if their opponents are doing even better. In 1980 Senator Kennedy found that President Carter was outspending him in virtually every state, including his home state of Massachusetts (New Hampshire was one exception). That same year, Bush was forced to take out a bank loan of $2.8 million after losing to Reagan in several primaries.

Candidates must decide not only how to raise funds but also how to spend them. The overall spending limits for the entire campaign ($17.6 million in 1980 and $24.4 million in 1984), as well as expenditure limits in each state, require that money be carefully allocated. Because they want to win in initial primaries and caucuses, candidates are inclined to spend heavily in the very early stage of the campaign. By February 26, 1980, the date of the New Hampshire primary, Reagan had spent two-thirds of his allowable limit for the entire campaign consisting of thirty-four Republican primaries.[18] Figure 2-1 shows that Mondale expended a major portion

Figure 2-1 Cumulative Proportions of Each Democratic Candidate's Total Expenditures and Delegates Apportioned over Time, 1983-1984 (Percent)

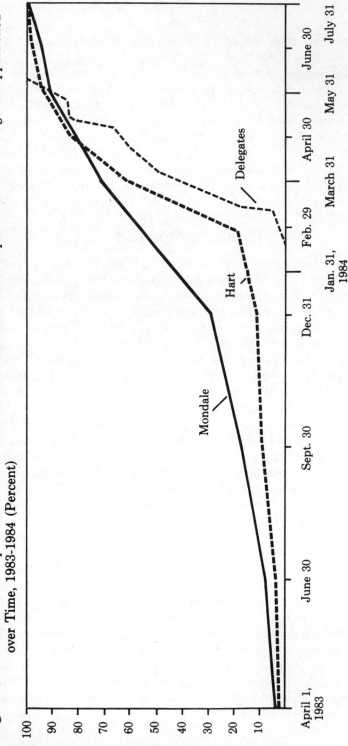

Source: Gary R. Orren, "The Nomination Process: Vicissitudes of Candidate Selection," in *The Elections of 1984*, ed. Michael Nelson (Washington, D.C.: CQ Press, 1985), 48.
Note: Excludes fund-raising expenditures.

of his funds before the delegate selection process began in February 1984, while Hart's spending was more in proportion to the number of delegates at stake.

Summary of Developments in Recent Nomination Campaigns

As the elements of campaigning, discussed in the preceding sections, suggest, presidential nomination campaigns are highly complex operations that call for a variety of specialists. Pollsters help candidates assess their nomination prospects and provide vital feedback on the reactions of voters to the candidates and their campaigns, on the issues that people are thinking about, and on the attitudes of social and economic groups about such issues. Media consultants help candidates develop a favorable image, write their speeches, and plan their television appearances. Direct-mail specialists help raise money and get out the vote. Since the 1952 presidential election, candidates have turned more and more to political consultants to organize these diverse operations, to develop strategy, and to manage the overall campaign.

Since the late 1960s control over the fate of presidential candidates has passed from a relatively few party professionals to rank-and-file voters. The attitudes of these voters evolve during the course of the nomination contest, in large part because of the influence of the media. In the early stages of the contest the media help determine who the viable candidates are; then, once the state primaries and caucuses begin, they label the "winners" and "losers," often, thereby, influencing the results of future state contests, for voters gravitate toward the winners and desert the losers. Periodic public opinion polls reflect the presidential preferences of U.S. voters, as do the results of state primaries and caucuses.

Moreover, the attitudes of voters, the media, the polls, and the state contest results influence one another. Candidates who receive favorable treatment from the media tend to do well in the primaries, and their showing there, in turn, raises their standings in the polls. Favorable polls impress representatives of the media as well as political activists and many rank-and-file voters, leading to more victories for the poll leaders in both nonprimary and primary contests. The result of this reinforcement process is that by the time the delegates gather for their party's national convention, one candidate usually has emerged. This candidate has received the most extensive and the most favorable media coverage, has led in the polls, and has won more primary and caucus-convention contests than any other candidate.[19] However, one more hurdle remains for the front-runner to cross—the party's national convention.

The National Convention

The national convention is important to presidential candidates for two reasons. First, whatever may have happened before, the actual nomination occurs at the convention. Second, the convention provides opportunities for candidates to strengthen their chances to win the general election the following November.

Rules and Politics of the Proceedings

Several decisions that precede the balloting for the nomination can affect significantly both the choice of nominee and the outcome of the general election. Sometimes the location of the convention is important. (The party's national committee officially makes this decision: for the party out of power, the national committee chairperson has the greatest say in the matter; for the party in power, the U.S. president does.) The welcoming speech of Illinois governor Adlai Stevenson to the Democratic delegates assembled in Chicago in 1952 is credited with influencing their decision to nominate him that year. In 1968 the confrontation in Chicago between protestors and Mayor Daley's police contributed to Hubert Humphrey's defeat in the general election.

Also important are the struggles between rival slates of delegates from states where the process of selecting delegates was disputed. At the 1952 Republican convention, the Credentials Committee awarded Robert Taft a majority of the delegates in several southern states, but this decision was overturned on the floor of the convention in favor of the ultimate nominee, Dwight Eisenhower. At the 1972 Democratic convention, there were eighty-two separate challenges involving thirty states and more than 40 percent of the delegates; most of the disputes stemmed from alleged violations of the McGovern Commission guidelines. Eventually, all but two were settled by the Credentials Committee; these went to the convention floor and were resolved in Senator McGovern's favor. He was awarded all of California's delegate votes even though, as previously noted, he won only 45 percent of that state's primary vote. Another dispute led to a convention decision to seat the delegation favoring the senator, not the regular Illinois delegation linked with Mayor Daley of Chicago, on the grounds that the latter did not contain an adequate representation of youth, women, and minorities and was chosen through improper processes.

Fights over rules of convention proceedings sometimes take on great significance. One such battle occurred at the 1976 Republican convention when the Reagan forces moved to amend the rules so as to require candidates to name their vice-presidential choice before the balloting on presidential candidates; they hoped thereby to force Ford to name a running mate and thus risk the loss of supporters who would be disappointed with his decision. (Before the convention Reagan had chosen liberal-to-moderate Pennsylvania senator Richard Schweiker as his vice president, a move calculated to bring him needed support from uncommitted delegates in large eastern states such as New York and Pennsylvania.) The defeat of that amendment helped pave the way for President Ford's victory on the first ballot that year. In 1980 Edward Kennedy's forces attempted to persuade the Democratic convention delegates to vote down a rule, first proposed by the Winograd Commission and later adopted by the Democratic National Committee, that required delegates to vote on the first ballot for a presidential candidate to whom they were pledged in their home state's primary or caucus-convention. When the convention upheld the rule, the Massachusetts senator knew he had no chance of winning the Democratic nomination, for more than a majority of the delegates were pledged to Carter. Kennedy immediately withdrew his candidacy on the very first night of the convention.

Writing and adopting the party platform entails other important convention decisions. Although critics traditionally have ridiculed the platforms for containing promises the party does not intend to keep, presidents of both parties have used their influence to enact the promises into law.[20] Moreover, many delegates and party leaders take them seriously.[21] In 1948 some of the delegates to the Democratic convention felt that the platform was too liberal on civil rights; twenty years later the Democrats bitterly debated the Vietnam plank of the platform. Republicans also have experienced major conflicts over their party platform: in 1964 the conservative Goldwater forces, which controlled that convention, refused to make any concessions to party moderates, such as governors Nelson Rockefeller of New York and George Romney of Michigan, on civil rights and political extremism.

One of the problems of platform fights is that the intraparty conflict may influence the general election campaign. Some southerners formed a third party in 1948 (the States' Rights party headed by South Carolina governor J. Strom Thurmond), which actually carried four southern states—Alabama, Louisiana, Mississippi, and South Carolina. Republican governors Nelson Rockefeller and George Romney did little to help Goldwater in 1964, and many Democrats opposed to the proadministration plank on Vietnam in the party's 1968 platform did not rouse themselves in the general election campaign that year.

Because of the possibility of splitting the party in the fall campaign, presidential candidates and their supporters sometimes decide not to fight their major rivals over the platform. After defeating Ronald Reagan for the 1976 Republican nomination, President Ford allowed the views of the California governor to prevail on several major provisions of the platform, including advocating a "moral" foreign policy (in contrast to détente, the policy the Ford administration had pursued with the Soviet Union). In 1980 President Carter followed a similar procedure in permitting the Kennedy forces to add to the Democratic platform a provision for a $12-billion, antirecession job program. In 1984 Mondale allowed Hart to add a plank spelling out the conditions under which a Democratic president would use U.S. forces abroad and Jackson to add one providing for "affirmative action goals and timetables and other verifiable measurements."

Credentials contests, the adoption of rules of procedure, and the writing of the party platform are tests of strength for the candidates and often determine who will prevail in the most important decision of the convention—the balloting for president, which typically takes place on the third day of the proceedings. In the interim, preparations are made for the roll call vote. Presidential hopefuls frequently call on caucuses of state delegations and sometimes contact individual delegates for their support. Polls are taken of delegates so that candidates know how many votes they can count on and from whom they may pick up additional support. In 1960 Edward Kennedy retained contacts with the Wyoming delegates he had worked with the previous spring and was in their midst when his brother won the nomination on the first ballot.[22] Also in 1960, Richard Nixon arranged to have his picture taken with each delegate at the Republican convention.[23]

The strategy a candidate employs in the balloting depends on the amount of delegate support he has. If he is the front-runner, as President Ford asserted he was in 1976, he concentrates on holding the votes he has been promised and on picking up any additional votes needed to win a majority on the initial ballot. The candidate and his workers use the bandwagon technique to achieve this goal—that is, they argue that since he will win the nomination anyway, delegation chairpersons or individual members who are politically smart will come out at that time for his candidacy rather than wait until the matter has already been settled. The candidate, the workers imply, will remember early support in the future when he is in a position to do political favors. Franklin Roosevelt did so quite specifically after he was elected in 1932: he determined whether a person seeking a political position had backed him "before Chicago" (where the convention had been held).

Candidates with less delegate support attempt to counter the bandwagon technique with their own strategies. They try to create the impression that the nomination is still uncertain, as the Reagan forces did at the 1976 Republican convention. At times, they may encourage delegates who do not support them to cast their ballots for favorite sons or other minor candidates; their objective is to hold down the vote for the front-runner on the first roll call. Candidates also attempt to forge alliances to stop the leader. They may agree, for example, that at some time during the balloting, those who fall behind in the voting will throw their support to others. The difficulty with making such an arrangement is that minor candidates frequently have greater differences among themselves than they have with the leader. The only alliance that conceivably might have stopped Richard Nixon at the 1968 Republican convention would have been one between Nelson Rockefeller and Ronald Reagan. However, given their divergent views on vital issues of the day, and Rockefeller's failure to support Goldwater in 1964 (Reagan had made the best speech of that campaign on Goldwater's behalf), the two governors were hardly a compatible political combination.

The leader, along with other candidates, offers various enticements in bargaining with possible political supporters. Some people are interested in persuading the party to take a particular stand on the platform. Others have more tangible concerns: senators or governors may seek the candidate's support in their own campaigns; other political leaders may be looking toward a cabinet post. Although a presidential candidate himself may refuse to make such commitments so that he can go before his party and the electorate as a "free" man beholden to no one, his supporters do not hesitate to make promises. One delegate to the 1960 convention claimed to be the nineteenth person to whom the Kennedy forces had offered the vice presidency.[24]

A definite trend in recent conventions is early victory for the candidate who arrives at the convention with the greatest number of pledged delegates. In the twenty conventions the two major parties have held since World War II, only two nominees—Thomas Dewey in 1948 and Adlai Stevenson in 1952—failed to win a majority of the convention votes on the first ballot. Thus, the convention has become a body that typically legitimizes the decision on the presidential nominee that has already been made by the time the delegates gather to choose a candidate officially.

The selection of the vice-presidential nominee is the final decision of the convention. Although in theory the delegates make the choice, as a matter of political custom they allow presidential nominees to pick their own running mates. On rare occasions nominees may decide against expressing their preferences and permit the convention to make an open choice, as Adlai Stevenson did in 1956. The typical presidential nominee, however, confers with leaders whose judgment he trusts, and, when he makes the decision, the word is passed on to the delegates. Even though some delegates may resist a particular vice-presidential candidate, nominees generally get their way. In 1940 Franklin Roosevelt threatened to refuse the presidential nomination unless Henry Wallace were chosen as his vice president. In 1960 John Kennedy insisted on Lyndon Johnson as his running mate over the objections of some liberal members of the party, including his brother Robert. In effect, the vice president is the first political appointment of the winning presidential nominee.

Various considerations underlie the choice of a vice-presidential candidate. Parties traditionally attempt to balance the ticket—that is, to select a person who differs in certain ways from the presidential nominee. For example, the two candidates may come from separate parts of the country. Over the years, the Democratic party often has chosen southerners to run with presidential nominees who were typically from other, two-party areas; the Kennedy-Johnson ticket in 1960 was such a combination. In 1976, when a southerner, Jimmy Carter, won the Democratic presidential contest for the first time since before the Civil War, the process worked in reverse; he chose Walter Mondale from the northern state of Minnesota as his running mate. In 1972 George McGovern originally chose Sen. Thomas Eagleton as his running mate, because the Missourian possessed certain characteristics the South Dakotan lacked: affiliation with the Roman Catholic church, ties to organized labor, and previous residence in a large city (St. Louis). In 1980 Ronald Reagan chose George Bush (whom he reportedly did not much admire personally) in order to win the support of moderates in the Republican party. In 1984 Mondale selected as his running mate Rep. Geraldine Ferraro of New York, who not only complemented the ticket geographically but also was the first woman and first Italian-American to serve as a major party candidate in a presidential contest. The ticket is balanced in these ways to broaden its appeal and thereby strengthen the party's chances in the general election.

Some presidential nominees, however, at least consider how the vice-presidential candidate will perform in office. The trend toward assigning important responsibilities to the second in command has led some candidates to choose running mates with whom they feel they can work effectively. This was the main reason Carter chose Walter Mondale over other northern liberal senators he had interviewed for the position, including Edmund Muskie of Maine, Frank Church of Idaho, John Glenn of Ohio, and Adlai Stevenson III of Illinois. The possibility of succession also has led presidents to choose the running mate who seems most able to assume the duties of the nation's highest office. John Kennedy reportedly chose Lyndon Johnson not only because he balanced the Democratic ticket in 1960 but also because Kennedy considered the Texan to be the most capable leader among his rivals for the presidential nomination.

Whatever the considerations that prompt the choice of a running mate, there is no doubt that presidential nominees often make the decision too quickly, and frequently without complete knowledge of the candidate's background. A notable example is McGovern's choice of Eagleton in 1972. McGovern and his staff met the morning after his nomination (many of them having had only two or three hours of sleep), and by five o'clock that afternoon they finally settled on Eagleton. The Missourian accepted the nomination after several other persons had either turned it down, could not be contacted, or were vetoed by key McGovern supporters. During that time no one turned up the information on Eagleton's history of mental illness, which ultimately led McGovern to force him off the ticket.

After the vice-presidential candidate is chosen, the final night of the convention proceedings is given over to acceptance speeches. On this occasion the presidential nominee tries to reunite the candidates and various party elements that have confronted one another during the long preconvention campaign and the hectic days of the convention. Major party figures usually come to the convention stage and pledge their support for the winner in the upcoming campaign. At times, however, personal feelings run too high and wounds fail to heal sufficiently for a show of party unity. In 1964, for example, important members of the liberal wing of the Republican party did not support the GOP standard-bearer, Barry Goldwater; and in 1968 many McCarthyites among Democrats (including McCarthy himself) refused to endorse the chosen nominee, Hubert Humphrey, at least immediately. In 1972 prominent Democratic leaders, including George Meany of the AFL-CIO, did not support McGovern. Senator Kennedy and many of his followers did not enthusiastically endorse President Carter on the final night of the 1980 Democratic convention. Thus, the convention does not always achieve one of its main objectives: to rally the party faithful for the general election battle.

Recent Changes in Conventions

The principal activities of today's national conventions are the same as those developed one and a half centuries ago: devising the rules of

55

procedure, adopting platforms, and, most important, nominating presidential and vice-presidential candidates. Recent developments, however, particularly since the mid-1960s, have radically changed the character of party conventions.

The most basic change is the way political power is organized and exercised at the convention. In the past, to win their party's nomination, presidential candidates were forced to negotiate with party leaders, particularly with those who chaired state delegations (often governors).[25] Today, however, candidates' personal organizations dominate the convention proceedings and contact individual delegates directly rather than working through the leaders who chair state delegations. Thus the growth in importance of candidate (rather than party) organizations, which has occurred in presidential nomination campaigns, has carried over into the national convention itself.

The character of convention delegates also changed in the late 1960s and 1970s. Students of those conventions have identified a basic split in both parties between amateur and professional delegates; the former are motivated primarily by candidates' stands on the issues, the latter by their ability to unite the party and win in November.[26] In the 1980s, however, the distinction between the two types of delegates has blurred as former amateurs share power with professionals and take on many of the latter's characteristics. Two political scientists call these people the "new professionals." [27]

Also becoming more prominent are delegate caucuses that transcend state boundaries, such as those organized by women, blacks, and Chicanos. In some instances these groups take the leadership in platform fights, as women did at the 1976 Republican convention over the ratification of the Equal Rights Amendment (ERA) and at the 1980 Democratic convention over the use of Medicaid funds for abortions and the denial of financial and technical campaign support to candidates not supporting ERA. Also surfacing as power blocs are those organized by interest groups: the AFL-CIO had 405 delegates and the National Education Association 302 delegates at the 1980 Democratic convention.[28]

Finally, technological developments have affected recent nominating conventions. Sophisticated electronic equipment enables centralized candidate organizations to communicate directly with their organizers and with individual delegates on the crowded convention floor. Even more important is the mass media's thorough and immediate coverage of convention proceedings. Such coverage has forced the parties to stage proceedings in a way that appeals to a nationwide audience; visually important events must be scheduled to take advantage of prime-time viewing. The media's close attention also has made it difficult for the parties to carry on delicate negotiations. As columnist David Broder has pointed out, not since 1952 (when, he suggests, television "took over" the convention hall) has either major party used more than one ballot to nominate its presidential candidate. He attributes this consequence to the party members' inability "to take the time for the slow and sometimes secretive bargaining that in the past allowed their national conventions to function successfully as coalition-building institutions." [29] Some observers of the 1980 Republican convention believe that the reason the GOP failed to consummate the "dream ticket" of Reagan and Ford was the media's relentless pressure to cover and thereby even to shape the delicate negotiations surrounding that important decision.

Notes

1. Austin Ranney, "Changing the Rules of the Nominating Game," in *Choosing the President,* ed. James David Barber (Englewood Cliffs, N.J.: Prentice-Hall, 1974), 71.
2. Arthur Hadley, *The Invisible Primary* (Englewood Cliffs, N.J.: Prentice-Hall, 1976).
3. Jules Witcover, "Sen. Mondale Won't Seek Presidential Nomination," *Washington Post,* November 22, 1974, A1.
4. Theodore H. White, *The Making of the President, 1972* (New York: Bantam, 1973), 127.
5. Martin Schram, *Running for President 1976: The Carter Campaign* (New York: Stein and Day, 1977), 8.
6. Donald Matthews, "Presidential Nominations: Process and Outcomes," in *Race for the Presidency: The Media and the Nominating Process,* ed. James David Barber (Englewood Cliffs, N.J.: Prentice-Hall, 1978), 39.
7. John Aldrich, *Before the Convention: A Theory of Presidential Nomination Campaigns* (Chicago: University of Chicago Press, 1980), 70.
8. Schram, *Running for President,* 20.
9. Former Tennessee senator Howard Baker noted that this development has made the Iowa caucuses the "functional equivalent of a primary" (Lou Cannon and William Peterson, "GOP," in *The Pursuit of the Presidency,* ed. Richard Harwood [New York: Berkeley, 1980], 129).
10. Michael W. Traugott, "The Media and the Nominating Process," in *Before Nomination: Our Primary Problems,* ed. George Grassmuck (Washington, D.C.: American Enterprise Institute, 1985), 111-112.
11. Timothy Crouse, *The Boys on the Bus* (New York: Ballentine Books, 1972).
12. Thomas Patterson, *The Mass Media Election: How Americans Choose Their President* (New York: Praeger, 1980), chap. 3.
13. Television reporters refer to coverage of candidates arriving at and departing from airports as "here he comes, there he goes" stories.
14. Patterson, *Mass Media Election,* chap. 4.

15. Ibid., 44.
16. William C. Adams, "Media Coverage of Campaign '84: A Preliminary Report," *Public Opinion,* April-May, 1984, 10-11, cited in Gary R. Orren, "The Nomination Process: Vicissitudes of Candidate Selection," in *The Elections of 1984,* ed. Michael Nelson (Washington, D.C.: CQ Press, 1985), 53.
17. Jeane Kirkpatrick, *The New Presidential Elite: Men and Women in National Politics* (New York: Russell Sage Foundation and the Twentieth Century Fund, 1976).
18. Cannon and Peterson, "GOP," 128.
19. Recent exceptions to that trend, when two candidates ended the preconvention period fairly even in those respects, are: Ford and Reagan in 1976, McGovern and Humphrey in 1972, and Mondale and Hart in 1984.
20. Gerald Pomper and Susan Lederman, *Elections in America: Control and Influence in Democratic Politics,* 2d ed. (New York: Longman, 1980), chap. 8.
21. Judith Parris, *The Convention Problem: Issues in Reform of Presidential Nominating Procedures* (Washington, D.C.: Brookings, 1972), 110.
22. Theodore H. White, *The Making of the President, 1960* (New York: Pocket Books, 1961), 203.
23. Nelson Polsby and Aaron Wildavsky, *Presidential Elections: Strategies of American Electoral Politics* (New York: Scribners, 1964), 82.
24. Ibid., 4th ed. (1976), 144.
25. Robert Peabody, Norman Ornstein, and David Rohde, "The United States Senate as a Presidential Incubator: Many Are Called but Few Are Chosen," *Political Science Quarterly* (Summer 1976): 248.
26. Robert Robach, "Amateurs and Professionals: Delegates to the 1972 Republican National Convention," *Journal of Politics* (May 1975): 436-469; John Soule and Wilma McGrath, "A Comparative Study of Presidential Nominations: The Democrats, 1968 and 1972," *American Journal of Political Science* (August 1975): 501-517; Robert Nakamura, "Beyond Purism and Professionalism: Styles of Convention Delegate Followership," *American Journal of Political Science* (May 1980): 207-232.
27. William Crotty and John S. Jackson III, *Presidential Primaries and Nominations* (Washington, D.C.: CQ Press, 1985), 122.
28. Michael Malbin, "The Conventions, Platforms, and Issue Activists," in *The American Elections of 1980,* ed. Austin Ranney (Washington, D.C.: American Enterprise Institute, 1981), 128.
29. David Broder, "Political Reporters in Presidential Politics," in *Inside the System,* ed. Charles Peters and John Rothchild, 2d ed. (New York: Praeger, 1973), 7.

Selected Readings

Aldrich, John. *Before the Convention: A Theory of Presidential Nomination Campaigns.* Chicago: University of Chicago Press, 1980.
Crouse, Timothy. *The Boys on the Bus.* New York: Ballentine Books, 1972.
Hadley, Arthur. *The Invisible Primary.* Englewood Cliffs, N.J.: Prentice-Hall, 1976.
Patterson, Thomas. *The Mass Media Election: How Americans Choose Their President.* New York: Praeger, 1980.

Election Rules and the Election Campaign ══ 3

As the quest for the presidency shifts from the nomination to the election phase, candidates face new political problems. The rules change, because the electoral college and the campaign finance legislation pertaining to general elections shape the way the fall campaign will be waged. New political appeals must be developed for this new stage of the campaign, now essentially a one-on-one contest, pitting the nominees of the two major parties against each other (although, on occasion, a strong third party candidate may run). The audience of the campaign increases greatly—about twice as many people vote in the general election as participate in the nomination process. Candidates and staff members therefore must decide how they can win the support of these new voters as well as appeal to persons generally identifying with the other party who backed losing candidates in the nomination process. A further complication is the length of the campaign: this new, expanded phase of the presidential contest is compressed into a mere ten weeks, roughly Labor Day to election day.

The first section of this chapter traces the evolution of the electoral college system and explains how it and recent campaign finance laws affect the general election campaign. The second section analyzes the campaign in the same framework as was used in Chapter 1 for the nomination contest: its early stages and targeting efforts, the kinds of political appeals that are directed toward the electorate, the communication of these appeals through the media and campaign workers, and the sources and types of expenditures.

Rules of the Election Contest

The two major rules affecting the general election are (1) the constitutional requirement that the electoral college choose the president and

(2) campaign finance laws. They help to determine how and where the fall campaign will be conducted.

The Electoral College

The method of selecting the president was among the most difficult problems the delegates to the Constitutional Convention faced.[1] A variety of plans were proposed, the two most important being selection by the Congress and direct election by the people. The first, derived from the practice in most states of the legislature's choosing the governor, had the backing of a number of delegates, including Roger Sherman of Connecticut. It was eventually discarded because of fear of legislative supremacy and also because the delegates could not choose between state-unit voting, which favored the small states, and joint action of the two chambers, which benefited the large states with their greater voting power in the House of Representatives. Three of the most influential members of the convention—James Madison of Virginia and James Wilson and Gouverneur Morris of Pennsylvania—supported direct popular election, but most delegates considered it too democratic. As George Mason of Virginia said, "It would be as unnatural to refer the choice of a proper magistrate to the people as it would to refer a trial of colors to a blind man."

Having decided against both popular election and selection by legislative bodies, the delegates proceeded to adopt an entirely new plan put forth by one of their own committees. The proposal, which some historians believe was based on a method used in Maryland to elect state senators, specified that each state legislature could choose electors, by whatever means it desired, equal to its total number of senators and representatives in Congress but that none of the electors could be members of Congress or hold other national office.[2] The individual electors would assemble at a fixed time in their respective state capitals and cast two votes each for president. These votes were then to be transmitted to Washington, D.C., where they would be opened and counted during a joint session of Congress. Whoever received the largest number of electoral votes would be declared president, provided a majority (one more than half) had been obtained; if no candidate received a majority, the House of Representatives, voting by states (one state delegation, one vote), would choose the president from among the five candidates receiving the highest number of electoral votes. After the president was chosen, the person with the next highest number of electoral votes would be declared vice president. If two or more contenders received an equal number of electoral votes, the Senate would choose the vice president from among them.

This complicated procedure reflected values and assumptions about human nature enunciated in *The Federalist Papers*. (The particular selection, Number 68, is attributed to Alexander Hamilton, whose views were somewhat more elitist than those of the majority of the delegates to the Constitutional Convention.) The Founders felt that the average person did not have the ability to make sound judgments about the qualifications of the presidential candidates and that this crucial decision therefore should be left to a small group of electors—a political elite who would have both the information and the wisdom necessary to choose the best persons for the nation's two highest offices. Because the electors could not be national officeholders with connections to the president, they could approach their task without bias; because they assembled separately in their respective state capitals rather than as a single body, there would be less chance of their being corrupted or exposed to popular unrest. Moreover, since they were convened .for a single purpose and would be dissolved when their task was completed, the possibility of tampering with them in advance or rewarding them with future favors was eliminated.

Philosophy shaped the presidential selection process adopted by the delegates, but so did a recognition of political factors. One student of the subject suggests that some of the delegates did not expect the electors to be entirely insulated from popular preferences.[3] They anticipated that each state's electors would cast one vote for a "native son," a locally popular political figure, and the other for a "continental character," an individual with a national reputation that members of the political elite would be aware of, even though the person might not be well known to the average citizen. (Evidence for this assumption is provided by Article II, Section 1, of the Constitution, which states that at least one of the two persons for whom an elector votes must not be an inhabitant of the elector's state.)

The Founders also expected that after George Washington's presidency, the electoral votes would be so widely distributed that few candidates would receive a majority, and, therefore, most elections (Mason estimated about nineteen out of twenty) would ultimately be decided by the House of Representatives. The electors would thus serve to "screen" (or, in today's terms, "nominate") the candidates, and the House would choose (elect) the president from among them. The conflict between large and small states, which was settled by the Connecticut Compromise on the composition of the Senate and House, also arose in the plan the delegates worked out for the selection of the chief executive. In the initial vote by the electors, the large states had the advantage, because the number of each state's votes reflected the size of its House delegation. If no candidate got a majority, the small states were favored in the second selection, because the contingent vote was by states, not by the number of representatives.

As was true of so many issues decided by the Founders, the method of selecting the president was a compromise. In addition to resolving the large-state/small-state conflict, the electoral college device took into account the attitudes of the advocates of states' rights by allowing the state legislatures to decide how the electors should be chosen. It also held open, for those who favored letting the people choose the president, the possibility of the electors' actually reflecting the popular vote for the president in their state. As political scientist John Roche has pointed out, the intermediate elector scheme gave "everybody a piece of the cake"; he also notes, however, that "the future was left to cope with the problem of what to do with this Rube Goldberg mechanism." [4]

Events soon nullified both the philosophical and political assumptions underlying the Founders' vision of the electoral college and forced them to cope with the "Rube Goldberg mechanism." The formation and organization of political parties in the 1790s proceeded so quickly that by the election of 1800, the electors no longer served as independent persons exercising their own judgments on candidates' capabilities; instead, they acted as agents of political parties and the general public. In 1800, the Republican party was so disciplined that all Republican electors cast their two votes for Thomas Jefferson and Aaron Burr. Although it was generally understood that Jefferson was the Republican candidate for president and Burr the candidate for vice president, the Constitution provided no means for the electors to make that distinction on their ballots. The result was a tie in electoral votes; neither won a majority, and the matter was handed to the House of Representatives for a final decision. Ironically, the Federalists, despite their major defeat in the congressional elections of 1800, still controlled the lame-duck Congress (which did not expire until March 1801) and therefore were in a position to help decide which Republican would serve as president and which as vice president. At the urging of Alexander Hamilton, who disagreed with Jefferson on policy matters but distrusted Burr personally, some of the Federalist representatives eventually cast blank ballots, which permitted the Republican legislators to choose Jefferson as president on the thirty-sixth ballot.

One result of this bizarre chain of events was the ratification in 1804 of the Twelfth Amendment, stipulating that electors cast separate ballots for president and vice president. The amendment also provides that if no presidential candidate receives a majority of the electoral votes, the

House of Representatives, balloting by states, will select the president by majority vote from among the three (instead of five) candidates who receive the highest number of electoral votes. If no vice-presidential candidate receives a majority of electoral votes, similar procedures are to be used by the Senate in choosing between the two persons with the highest number of electoral ballots.

Other changes in the selection of the president followed; however, they did not come by way of constitutional amendments but as political developments that fit within the legal framework of the electoral college. Thus, state legislators, who were granted the power to determine how electors should be chosen, began giving this right to the general electorate. By 1832 all states except South Carolina had done so.

Another matter left to the discretion of the states—how their electoral votes would be counted—soon underwent change. States initially were inclined to divide the vote by congressional districts; the candidate who won the plurality (that is, more votes than anyone else) of the popular votes in each district received its electoral vote, and the remaining two electoral votes (representing the two Senate seats) were awarded to the statewide popular winner.

Legislatures soon, however, began to adopt the "unit" or "general-ticket" rule, whereby all the state's electoral votes went to the candidate who received the plurality of the statewide popular vote. Two political considerations prompted this decision. The state's majority party benefited because it did not have to award any electoral votes to a minority party that might be successful in individual congressional districts. Also, this system maximized the influence of the state in the presidential election by permitting it to throw all its electoral votes to one candidate. Once some states adopted this procedure, others, wanting to maintain their influence on the presidential contest, felt they had to follow. As a result, by 1836 the district plan had vanished, and the unit system had taken its place. (Since then, a few states have used the district plan, most recently Maine.)

Another political development of the era changed the nature of the presidential election contest: the elimination of property qualifications for voting. By the early 1840s white manhood suffrage was virtually complete in the United States. The increasing democratization of U.S. political life is reflected, therefore, in the procedure for choosing the most important public official. Yet, the formal provisions of the electoral college remain the same today as they were in 1804, when the Twelfth Amendment was adopted.

Today these formal provisions provide a strange system for choosing the chief executive. Although most Americans view the system as a popular election, it really is not. When voters mark their ballots for a presidential candidate, the vote is actually cast for the electors who are linked with that candidate. In mid-December the state electors associated with the winning candidate (party faithfuls who are chosen in primaries, at conventions, or by state committees) meet in their state capitals to vote. (About one-third of the states attempt by law to bind the electors to vote for the popular-vote winner, but there is some question whether such laws are constitutional.) The results of the electoral balloting are transmitted to Washington, D.C.; on the following January 6 they are counted, and the presiding officer of the Senate, who is the incumbent vice president, announces the outcome before a joint session of the Congress. If, as usually happens, one candidate receives a majority of the electoral votes, the vice president officially declares that candidate to be president, a procedure that occasionally has created some ironic moments. In January 1961, Richard Nixon declared his opponent, John Kennedy, to be president; eight years later another vice president, Hubert Humphrey, declared his opponent, this time Richard Nixon, to be the chief executive.

The electoral college system as it operates today is considered by many students of presidential elections to be not only strange but also grossly unfair; some even consider it dangerous. Chapter 5 assesses the arguments for and against the electoral college; this section examines only the effects the present arrangements have on campaign strategies.

Under the electoral college system, election results are decided state by state. All the states except Maine use the unit or general-ticket system, which means that all the electoral votes of a state go to the candidate who wins a mere plurality of its popular votes. Thus, in effect, there are fifty separate presidential contests with a "winner-take-all" principle that puts a premium on a popular vote victory in each state, no matter how small the margin of that victory may be.

A built-in bias in the electoral college works to the advantage of certain states over others. The present system benefits the very small and the very large states. The small states have the advantage of what political scientist Lawrence Longley calls the "constant two" votes, that is, the two electoral votes, representing the two senators, that all states receive, regardless of size.[5] This arrangement—the constant two, plus the additional vote for their House member—means that the smallest states control three electoral votes, even though their population alone might entitle them to just one or two votes. The very large states have an even greater advantage; they benefit from the unit or general-ticket system because all their electoral votes are awarded to their popular-vote winner. Thus in 1984 the popular-vote winner in California (Ronald Reagan) received 47 electoral votes, almost 18 percent of the total 270 electoral votes required for election.[6] (See Figure 3-1 for an illustration of the size of the states based on their number of electoral votes for the 1984 election, which reflect changes occasioned by the 1980 census.)

Longley also shows that residency in the very small and the very large states of the Far West and, to a lesser extent, the East is an advantage for some ethnic groups. Voters who are concentrated in urban areas, both central cities and the suburbs, also benefit. In general, however, blacks are not among the ethnic groups who benefit by the rules of the system because the rules put the South, where many blacks live, at a disadvantage. (The South contains a disproportionate number of medium-sized states—those with from four to fourteen electoral votes. Medium-sized states offer candidates neither a great many electoral votes, as the big states do, nor a proportionately large number of electoral votes, as the small states do.)

Figure 3-1 State Size by Number of Electoral Votes, 1984

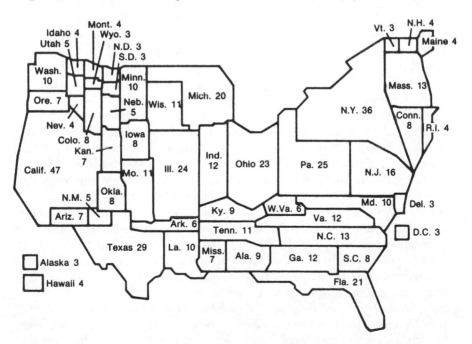

Note: To win, a candidate must receive 270 electoral votes.

Finally, the electoral college benefits certain kinds of candidates. These include not only those of the two major parties, who are in a position to win enough popular votes in a state to be awarded its electoral votes, but also third party candidates, who have a regional appeal sufficient to win some states. At a disadvantage, however, are third party candidates without that regional appeal. In 1948, Dixiecrat presidential candidate Strom Thurmond carried four states with a total of thirty-nine electoral votes, even though he won only about 2.4 percent of the national popular vote; that same year the Progressive party candidate, Henry Wallace, with the same percentage of the nationwide vote, did not carry any states and thus received no electoral votes at all.[7]

Rules Affecting Campaign Finance

The legal provisions for financing the general election differ considerably from those governing presidential nominations. For the general election, complete public financing is provided to nominees of the major parties (those that won 25 percent or more of the popular vote in the last presidential election). In the 1984 presidential election, the federal government gave each candidate $40.4 million and each national committee $6.9 million. But to be eligible for that money, nominees must agree not to accept other contributions to their campaign. Candidates of minor parties (those that won between 5 and 25 percent of the vote in the previous election) receive partial public financing. Candidates of parties ineligible for public financing (those that won less than 5 percent of the vote in the previous election) can be partially reimbursed after the current election if they receive at least 5 percent of that vote.

Two provisions of the campaign finance law permit the major party candidates to benefit from campaign expenditures besides those they make themselves from public funds. As is true of the nomination process, there is no limitation on independent campaign expenditures, that is, those made by individuals or political committees that advocate the defeat or election of a presidential candidate but that are not made in conjunction with the candidate's own campaign. (Again, however, such individuals and committees must file reports with the Federal Election Commission and must state under penalty of perjury that the expenditure was not made in collusion with the candidate.) In addition, an amendment to the campaign finance law enacted in 1979 permits state and local party organizations to spend money for any purpose except campaign advertising and the hiring of outside personnel; this means that they can engage in grass-roots activities such as distributing campaign buttons, stickers, and yard signs, registering voters, and transporting them to the polls to vote.

Thus, like the provisions for financing presidential nomination campaigns, those governing the general election have brought significant changes in the funding of fall presidential campaigns. The two major party candidates no longer need to depend on wealthy contributors and other private sources to finance their campaigns. (They may still benefit, however, from the independent expenditures of such sources as well as from grass-roots activities by state and local parties.) The law also has the effect of limiting and equalizing the expenditures made by the two major party candidates, which is a distinct advantage for the Democrats because, historically, Republican presidential candidates have spent more than their opponents.[8] (See Table 3-1, which shows that, except for 1948, the Republican presidential candidate outspent his Democratic opponent in every election from 1940 through 1972, the last contest before the enactment of the campaign finance law providing public funding.) Finally, the law benefits the candidates of the two major parties, who receive full public financing of their general election campaigns, in contrast to minor party candidates, who are entitled to only partial financing, if any at all.

The General Election Campaign

Traditionally, U.S. presidential campaigns have begun on Labor Day, but individual candidates are free to choose other times, depending on the political circumstances. Gerald R. Ford, seeking to reorganize his forces after a bruising battle with challenger Ronald Reagan at the 1976 Republican national convention, waited until a week after Labor Day to launch his fall campaign. In contrast, Ronald Reagan, with the Republican nomination locked up in both 1980 and 1984, hit the campaign trail early to counteract the favorable publicity generated by the Democratic national conventions of those two years. Thus the conditions under which candidates themselves win their party's nomination, plus the circumstances surrounding their opponent's choice, shape decisions on the beginning of the fall campaign.

Candidates also pay close attention to the locality of the first speech of the official campaign. Jimmy Carter chose two sites in his native South: in 1976, Warm Springs, Georgia (the city in his home state in which President Franklin D. Roosevelt died), and in 1980, Tuscumbia, Alabama. In 1980 Ronald Reagan selected Ellis Island in New York City harbor (the port of arrival for millions of immigrants seeking a new life in the United States), and in 1984, his original political base of Orange County, California.

Table 3-1 Cost of Presidential General Elections, 1940-1972
(Dollars in Millions)

Year	Republican		Democratic	
	Expenditure	Candidate	Expenditure	Candidate
1940	3.45	Willkie	2.78	F. Roosevelt*
1944	2.83	Dewey	2.17	F. Roosevelt*
1948	2.13	Dewey	2.74	Truman*
1952	6.61	Eisenhower*	5.03	Stevenson
1956	7.78	Eisenhower*	5.11	Stevenson
1960	10.13	Nixon	9.80	Kennedy*
1964	16.03	Goldwater	8.76	Johnson*
1968	25.40	Nixon*	11.59	Humphrey
1972	61.40	Nixon*	30.00	McGovern

Source: Excerpted from Herbert E. Alexander, *Financing Politics: Money, Elections and Political Reform* (Washington, D.C.: CQ Press, 1976), Table 2.1, 20.

Note: Asterisk (*) indicates winner.

Targeting the Campaign

As in the nomination process, presidential candidates must decide in which states they will focus their efforts in the fall campaign.[9] The decision is harder at this stage because the general election takes place simultaneously in all fifty states rather than in stages, and campaign efforts must be concentrated into a much shorter period of time than is available for the nomination campaign. Moreover, in the general election, unlike the nomination process, there are no legal limits on the amount of money presidential candidates can spend in individual states; they therefore have a freer hand in their choices, but those choices become more difficult.

By far the most important consideration in targeting the fall campaign is the electoral college. The candidate's goal is clear: to win the presidency, he or she must win a majority—270—of the 538 electoral votes. This fact places a premium on carrying those states with the largest number of electoral votes. In 1984, twelve of the largest states— California, New York, Texas, Pennsylvania, Illinois, Ohio, Florida, Michigan, New Jersey, North Carolina, Massachusetts, and either Georgia, Virginia, or Indiana (each has 12 electoral votes)—together had a total of 279 votes, enough to elect even a candidate who lost the thirty-eight other states. Naturally, candidates from both major political parties concentrate their personal visits on the largest states.

Another element that affects candidates' decisions on where to campaign is the political situation in a particular state; that is, whether the state generally goes to one party's candidate or whether it swings back and forth from one election to the next. Distinctly one-party states are likely to be slighted by both of the major party candidates. The party in control does not think it is necessary to waste time there. (In 1968 Nixon did not visit or spend money in Kansas; as one campaign aide, Robert Ellsworth, said of his home state, "If you have to worry about Kansas, you don't have a campaign anyway." [10]) In contrast, the opposition party is likely to think it futile to exert much effort in what is obviously enemy territory.[11] The "swing" states naturally draw the greatest attention from presidential candidates of both parties.

Since 1968, both major political parties have developed areas where their presidential candidates usually are successful. The Republicans have been strongest in the West; the Democrats have been strongest in the Northeast. The once-solid Democratic South has varied from election to election. The South was vital to the Democratic electoral strategies of Kennedy in 1960 and Carter in 1976 and helped to put both men in the White House. In contrast, Humphrey in 1968 and McGovern in 1972 wrote off the region, and the election results reflected this decision: Humphrey carried only Texas (considered by some political observers to be a western rather than a truly southern state), and McGovern did not win any states in the South.[12] Since 1968, however, Republican candidates have thought it worthwhile to contest the southern states, and Reagan even managed to defeat native son Jimmy Carter there in 1980. (The president carried only his home state of Georgia in that region and two border states, Maryland and West Virginia.) In 1984 Walter Mondale initially campaigned in a number of states in the South, but when it became apparent that he was not doing well there, he concentrated his efforts in Texas because of its twenty-nine electoral votes and large Mexican-American population, which has traditionally voted Democratic.

The regions that have been crucial in recent presidential contests are the Middle Atlantic states (New York, Pennsylvania, and New Jersey) and the Middle West states of Ohio, Michigan, Illinois, and Missouri. Together this tier of seven highly industrial states controlled 155 electoral votes in the 1984 election. They also tend to be highly competitive, which means that campaign efforts there can be very important in deciding which candidate prevails.

The most systematic plan in targeting a presidential campaign was developed for Jimmy Carter in 1976 by Hamilton Jordan. He assigned points to each state, using three criteria. The first was its number of electoral votes. The second was its Democratic potential based on the number of Democratic officeholders in the state and how well McGovern had done there in 1972. The third was how concerted a campaign was needed in a particular state, taking into account how well Carter had done in the preconvention period, how much time or resources he had previously expended in the state, and how close to Ford he was in the polls. Each campaigner was allocated points as well: for example, a day's campaigning by Carter was worth seven points; by Mondale, five points; and by a Carter child, one point. Jordan then assigned campaigners to states so that scheduling points were matched with those developed under the political-importance formula.[13]

Manipulating Political Appeals

Party Label. Political party labels, unimportant in the nomination process, become a focal point in general election campaigns. Given the Democrats' status as the majority party since the days of Franklin Roosevelt, it is natural that Democratic candidates throughout the years have emphasized their party affiliation and linked their opponents with the minority Republican party. In 1960 John Kennedy stressed that he "stood" with Woodrow Wilson, Franklin Roosevelt, and Harry S Truman, whereas his opponent, Richard Nixon, "stood" with William McKinley, William Howard Taft, Warren Harding, Alfred Landon, and Thomas Dewey. (Significantly, Kennedy did not mention popular Republican presidents such as Abraham Lincoln, Theodore Roosevelt, or Dwight D. Eisenhower.) Twenty years later Jimmy Carter pursued a similar strategy, emphasizing that he represented the party of Franklin Roosevelt, Harry Truman, John Kennedy, and Lyndon B. Johnson (leading Ronald Reagan to quip that the only Democratic president Carter was not talking about was himself). In 1984 Walter Mondale sought to link his candidacy with Truman, who, like Mondale, was counted out of the race by pollsters. In one appearance, Mondale held up the famous erroneous headline of the Chicago *Tribune,* "Dewey Defeats Truman."

Over the years, Republican presidential candidates have devised tactics to counteract the partisan advantage enjoyed by their Democratic opponents. One is to advise the voters to ignore party labels and vote for the "best man." Nixon used this approach in his 1960 campaign, urging Americans to cast their ballots for the person who had experience in foreign affairs, who had stood up to Soviet leader Nikita Khrushchev and bested him in a "kitchen debate" in Moscow. (The informal exchange over the comparative worth of communist and capitalist economic systems took place at a kitchen display at a fair in Moscow.) Another tactic is to suggest that the Democratic presidential candidate does not represent the views of the rank-and-file members of the party. In 1972

Nixon charged that the Democratic convention had rejected the historic principles of that party and implored, "To those millions who have been driven out of their home in the Democratic party, we say come home." Another ploy open to Republican presidential candidates is to associate themselves with past Democratic presidents. In 1976 Gerald Ford tied his candidacy to that of former Democratic chief executive Harry Truman, who, as an underdog incumbent, struggled successfully for the same goal as Ford: election to the office in his own right, not merely by succession. Four years later Reagan linked his desire for major changes in U.S. society with the New Deal, Fair Deal, and New Frontier administrations of Roosevelt, Truman, and Kennedy. In 1984 he participated in anniversary ceremonies for Roosevelt and Truman and held receptions at the White House in honor of Hubert Humphrey and former senator Henry Jackson.[14]

Whether a candidate represents the majority or the minority party, it is important that prominent political figures in the party support his campaign. In 1964 Barry Goldwater's candidacy suffered (although it is unlikely that he could have won the presidency in any event) because leading Republicans dissociated themselves from the party's presidential nominee and conducted independent campaigns of their own. Sen. Eugene McCarthy's lukewarm and belated endorsement of Hubert Humphrey in the last stages of the 1968 campaign did little to help Humphrey avert his narrow defeat that year. And in 1972 large numbers of Democratic candidates for congressional and state offices deliberately dissociated themselves from the McGovern-Shriver ticket.

Incumbency. Incumbent presidents who are running for reelection start out with certain advantages in the electoral contest. They are typically better known to the voters than their opponents, who must strive to narrow the recognition gap between the two candidates. The incumbent president frequently assumes the role of statesman, too busy with the affairs of the nation to participate in a demeaning, partisan campaign. Describing the 1972 contest between George McGovern and President Nixon, one journalist remarked, "Around the White House, it bordered on treason to call Nixon a candidate."[15] In 1976 Gerald Ford followed his advisers' recommendation by conducting the early stages of the campaign from the White House Rose Garden—gathering presidential publicity by receiving visitors, signing or vetoing bills, and calling press conferences to make announcements.

While the incumbent is operating above the partisan fray, others are free to make political attacks on the opposition. Frequently, the vice-presidential candidates assume that role, as Humphrey did for the

Democrats in 1964 and Robert Dole did for the Republicans in 1976.[16] Or the president's supporters may develop an entire team to carry on the effort. In 1972 the Committee to Reelect the President (note that Nixon's name did not even appear in the title of the committee) organized a special surrogate's office to schedule the campaign appearances of thirty-five White House aides, cabinet members, senators, representatives, mayors, and Republican party officials.

The incumbent president is also in a position to use the prerogatives of the office to good advantage during the election campaign. In 1976 President Ford suddenly recommended legislation to expand the national park system and to reduce the amount of down payments for mortgages guaranteed by the Federal Housing Administration. The president also can disburse forms of political "patronage" available to the nation's chief executive. In 1980 President Carter announced his support for water projects in Kentucky and Tennessee that he had previously opposed, offered the steel industry protection against foreign imports, approved financial aid to enable residents of Love Canal (the polluted area near Niagara Falls, New York) to move away from that region, and announced federally subsidized loans for drought-stricken farms. Even Chicago— whose mayor, Jane Byrne, supported Edward Kennedy in the primary fight—received its share of national government "goodies," which prompted Byrne to declare that while diamonds are still a girl's best friend, federal grants are next best. In 1984 President Reagan provided assistance to U.S. farmers by allowing the Soviet Union to purchase an extra 10 million metric tons of grain and by changing credit arrangements to grant greater relief to farmers who were heavily in debt.

Incumbent presidents can also use their office to publicize important events in foreign and military policy. During 1972 President Nixon visited both Communist China and the Soviet Union, gathering extensive media coverage in the process. In the spring of 1984, President Reagan went to China; in June of that year he journeyed to the Normandy beaches to lead the fortieth anniversary commemoration of the Allied invasion of France in World War II, an occasion attended by veterans and their families.

Candidate Image. Because the public focuses so much attention in a presidential campaign on the candidates themselves, the personality and character that the aspirants project are particularly important. Each campaign organization strives to create a composite image of the most attractive attributes of its candidate. Although the image necessarily deviates from reality, it must still reflect enough of the essential characteristics of the candidate to be believable. One effective tactic is to take a potential flaw and convert it into an asset. Thus, the somewhat elderly Dwight Eisenhower (he was aged sixty-six at the time of his second campaign in 1956) was pictured as a benevolent father (or even grandfather) whose mature judgment was needed to lead the nation in times of stress.[17] In contrast, the youthful John Kennedy, who was aged forty-three when he ran for the presidency in 1960, was characterized as a man of "vigor" who would make the United States "feel young again" after the Eisenhower years.

Presidential candidates frequently take their opponents' images into account when shaping their own. In 1976 Gerald Ford portrayed himself as a man of maturity and experience to counteract Jimmy Carter's emphasis on being a "new face" and an outsider to the Washington scene. Four years later as the incumbent president, Carter tried to come across as a deliberate and moderate person who could be trusted to maintain his calm in a crisis, in contrast to his supposedly impetuous and irresponsible opponent, Ronald Reagan. Reagan, in turn, presented himself as a decisive leader who could overcome the nation's problems, as opposed to Carter, depicted as an uncertain, vascillating person overwhelmed by the burdens of the presidency and inclined to blame the country's difficulties on the "spirit of malaise" of the American people themselves.

Besides molding their own images to balance those of their opponents, candidates also can directly attack the images of the opposition to put them in a bad light. In 1976, for example, Gerald Ford described Jimmy Carter as follows: "He wavers, he wanders, he wiggles, he waffles." He also charged that his opponent had a strange way of changing his accent: "In California he tried to sound like Cesar Chavez; in Chicago, like Mayor Daley; in New York, like Ralph Nader; in Washington, like George Meany; then he comes to the farm belt and he becomes a little old peanut farmer." During the second debate, after Ford stated that Eastern Europe was not under Soviet domination, Carter countered that the president must have been "brainwashed" when he went to Poland. (Carter was thereby comparing Ford with George Romney, the former Michigan governor whose nomination campaign collapsed in 1968 after he said he had been brainwashed by the military in the course of a trip to Vietnam.) The Georgian also said that during the second debate Ford had shown "very vividly the absence of good judgment, good sense, and knowledge" expected of a president. In 1980 Carter suggested that a Reagan presidency would divide Americans "black from white, Jew from Christian, North from South, rural from urban" and could "well lead our nation to war." Reagan, in turn, impugned Carter's honesty, saying that the president's promise that he would never lie to Americans reminded him of a quotation from Ralph Waldo Emerson, "The more he talked of his honor, the more we counted our spoons." In 1984, Walter Mondale was accused of being overly gloomy about the country and its prospects— "Whine on harvest moon," as Vice President George Bush liked to put it. Mondale and Geraldine Ferraro, in turn, attacked President Reagan for being the most "disengaged" president in recent history, one who lacked the knowledge necessary to govern the nation.

Social Groups. Fairly early in life many Americans begin to think of themselves as members of individual ethnic, geographic, or religious groups. As they get older, they also begin to identify with groups associated with their occupations and to consider themselves as businesspeople or farmers or members of labor unions. Sometimes people relate politically to groups to which they do not belong. A well-to-do white liberal, for example, who sympathizes with the underdog in society, may favor programs that benefit poor blacks. Responses to groups can also be negative: a self-made businessperson may have an unfavorable image of labor unions or social welfare organizations.

Presidential candidates take these group attitudes into account in devising campaign appeals. Since the days of Franklin Roosevelt, the Democratic party has aimed its campaigns at certain groups thought to be particularly susceptible to its political overtures: among these are southerners, blacks, members of ethnic groups, organized labor, Catholics, Jews, intellectuals, and big-city "bosses" and their political supporters (hence the quip that the Democratic party has more wings than a boardinghouse chicken). At the same time, the Democrats usually have tried to depict the Republicans as the party of "big business" and the rich.

Republican candidates have used explicit group appeals less often in their presidential campaigns. In fact, in 1964 Senator Goldwater conducted an antigroup campaign. The Republican candidate seemed to go out of his way to antagonize particular blocs, speaking in Knoxville against the Tennessee Valley Authority (TVA); in retirement communities such as St. Petersburg, Florida, against Social Security; and in Charleston, West Virginia, near the heart of Appalachia, against the Johnson administration's War on Poverty. (In writing off such groups as "minorities," Goldwater ignored the fact that an aggregation of minorities makes up a majority.) In 1968 Richard Nixon tried a different approach, aiming his campaign at the "forgotten Americans who did not break the law, but did pay taxes, go to work, school, church, and love their country." He thereby sought to establish a negative association between the Democrats and groups he considered to be outside the American mainstream, such as welfare recipients, atheists, and war protestors.

Some recent Republican presidential candidates, however, have been more inclined to seek the support of groups that traditionally have been sympathetic to the Democratic party. In 1972 the Committee to Reelect the President (Nixon) turned out campaign buttons for almost thirty nationalities, provided copy for ethnic newspapers and radio stations, and made special appeals to Catholics, Jews, blacks, and Mexican-Americans. In his 1980 presidential campaign Reagan appealed to union members by pointing out that he had been president of a labor union for six terms; courted the Polish vote by meeting on Labor Day with Stanislaw Walesa, father of the leader of the strike against the Polish government; and wooed blacks by arguing that their high unemployment rate was caused by the sluggish state of the economy. Four years later the Reagan campaign set aside an "ethnic week" to court groups such as Polish-Americans and Italian-Americans (recall that the Democratic vice-presidential candidate, Geraldine Ferraro, was the first person of Italian background to run for such a high office). Reagan also tried to appeal to Jews by criticizing Mondale for not repudiating Jesse Jackson's anti-Semitic remarks.

Two other groups took on a special significance in both 1980 and 1984. Women were thought to be anti-Reagan because of his promilitary stance and his opposition to social programs and the Equal Rights Amendment. Democrats played on such fears by portraying Reagan as "trigger-happy" and as insensitive to the needs of economic and social underdogs; the Republicans tried to assure women that he was a man of peace who looked to the private sector and state and local governments for financial assistance to the disadvantaged. The Republicans also appealed to fundamentalist Christians, particularly in the South, by advocating prayer in the public schools and by opposing abortion; Democrats tried to counter such appeals by arguing that prayers should be said in church and the home (not in school), and that the government also had no right to interfere with a woman's private decision whether or not to carry a pregnancy to term.

Another group of voters emerged in 1984 as a particular target for both political parties—young voters. Traditionally Democratic in their sympathies, college-age youth were wooed by Republican appeals of job opportunities in an expanding economy and love of country. The Democrats responded by appealing to the idealism of young people to help those less fortunate than themselves and to their concern about the dangers of nuclear war. As a result, both parties' candidates made many campaign appearances on college campuses (Mondale gave one of his best speeches at George Washington University), with both supporters and hecklers typically in attendance.

Issues and Events. Over the years, both major political parties have been associated with certain broad issues in American life. Democratic presidential candidates usually emphasize economic issues: by doing so they can link the Great Depression to the Republican president, Herbert Hoover, who was in office at the time, and they can draw on the voters' traditional preference of Democrats over Republicans to handle the economy. In contrast, Republican candidates focus more on foreign policy issues because Democratic presidents were in power at the start of World War I, World War II, and both the Korean and Vietnamese conflicts. As a result, many voters conclude that Republicans are better able to keep the peace than Democrats.

Circumstances surrounding particular elections can lead to changes in the traditional politics. In 1980 the poor economic record of the Carter administration led Ronald Reagan to focus on that issue; four years later, this time as the incumbent president, Reagan continued to emphasize the economy, because inflation and interest rates had fallen since he took office. In 1980 President Carter concentrated on foreign policy so that he could raise fears about Reagan's reliability in keeping the nation out of nuclear war. In 1984 Mondale pointed out that President Reagan was the first U.S. chief executive in the atomic era who had not met with a foreign chief of state to advance negotiations on an arms treaty.

Although candidates address major issues in U.S. society, they frequently do so only in very general terms. The party out of power often uses a catchy slogan to link the party in power with unfortunate political events. In 1952, for example, the Republicans branded the Democrats with "Korea, corruption, and communism." The party in power responds in the same way, as when the Democrats defended their record in 1952 by telling the voters, "You never had it so good." In 1976 the situation was reversed; Democrats talked about Watergate, inflation, unemployment, and President Ford's pardon of Richard Nixon. (Carter refused to attack Ford on the issue, but his vice-presidential candidate, Walter Mondale, did.) President Ford asserted that his administration had cut inflation by half, brought peace to the nation ("Not a single American is fighting or dying"), and restored faith, confidence, and trust in the presidency. In 1980, as in 1952, the Republicans attacked the Democratic incumbent: Ronald Reagan blamed President Carter for the nation's mounting economic problems and for allowing the United States to fall far behind the Soviet Union in military preparedness. At the same time the Democratic president pointed with pride to the signing of the Egyptian-Israeli accord, the ratification of the Panama Canal Treaty, and the development of an energy program.

This general sort of attack and defense characterizes most presidential campaigns. The party out of power blames all the ills of American life on the administration; the party in power maintains that all of the nation's blessings have resulted from its leadership. The candidate in the most difficult position is the nonincumbent nominee of the party in power, such as Nixon in 1960 and Humphrey in 1968. Both served as vice president in administrations whose policies they did not fully endorse. Nixon, for instance, did not believe Eisenhower was doing enough in space exploration and national defense. Humphrey opposed the bombing of North Vietnam when it was initiated in 1965. Yet each hesitated to criticize an administration in which he had served. Humphrey's inability to dissociate himself from the Johnson administration's Vietnam policy is considered one of the main reasons for his defeat in 1968.[18]

While addressing political issues only in very general terms, presidential candidates typically make few concrete proposals for dealing with such issues.[19] In 1960 Kennedy urged that he be given the chance to "get the nation moving again," but he was very vague about what, specifically, he would do to move the nation forward. Nixon was even more indefinite in 1968; he refused to spell out his plans for dealing with the most important U.S. political issue, Vietnam. His excuse was that doing so might jeopardize the Paris peace talks then being held.

In some presidential campaigns, however, candidates have made specific suggestions for dealing with issues. In 1972 George McGovern proposed that the defense budget be cut by 30 percent; and early in his campaign he advocated that everyone, regardless of need, be given a $1,000 grant by the government. In 1980 Reagan advocated the passage of the Kemp-Roth tax plan, which called for reducing taxes 10 percent each year over a period of three years. In 1984 Mondale unveiled a plan that called for cuts in defense, health, and agricultural expenditures and tax increases for upper-income earners and corporations so that by 1989 the budget deficit could be reduced by two-thirds.

In manipulating political appeals, candidates usually attempt to develop an all-encompassing theme that will give the voters an overall impression of the campaign. Sometimes the theme focuses on the candidates themselves, as did Humphrey's slogan, "He's a man you can trust"; the Carter-Mondale phrase, "Tested and trustworthy"; and Reagan's 1984 motto, "Leadership that's working." Or it may be essentially an appeal to a broad group, such as Nixon's "Forgotten Americans" who did not break the law but did pay their taxes, go to work, school, and church, and love their country. At other times the theme is directed at issues and political events ("Korea, corruption, and communism" or "peace and prosperity") or takes the form of a general call for action, such as Kennedy's "We've got to get the nation moving again"; McGovern's

"Come home, America"; Carter's promise to make the government as "truthful, capable, and filled with love as the American people"; and Reagan's 1980 invitation to a "new beginning." Once the theme is established, candidates try, by constant repetition, to get the electorate to respond emotionally to it. Their success in doing so depends, however, on another important aspect of presidential campaigns: how political appeals are communicated to the American voter.

Communicating with the Public

Because the electorate is twice as large as the selectorate and the campaign period for the election is much shorter than for the nomination, presidential candidates place even more emphasis on the mass media during this latter stage of the process. Advertising expenses are one measure of that emphasis: in the 1984 campaign, for example, Ronald Reagan and Walter Mondale each spent more than half of the $40 million subsidy from the federal government on television, radio, and print advertisements, with the lion's share spent on political commercials. Of these three types of media, television is by far the most important. It takes much less effort to watch than to read, particularly since viewing can be combined with other activities but reading cannot.[20] In addition, people are more inclined to believe what they see on television than what they read in the newspapers or hear on the radio. As a result, since 1952, television has been the chief source of campaign information for most Americans.

Over the years presidential candidates have employed several television formats. In 1968 Richard Nixon used sixty-second spot announcements during popular programs such as Rowan and Martin's "Laugh-in." The Republicans also staged appearances of Nixon before panels of citizens who asked questions that he could appear to answer spontaneously. (Nixon's advisers carefully screened both the panels and the questions to avoid possible embarrassment or surprise.)

In the 1972 campaign, the candidates adopted new formats for their televised political communications. Although spot commercials remained popular (one of Nixon's, for example, showed a hand sweeping away toy soldiers and miniature ships and planes to symbolize McGovern's proposed cuts in defense), five-minute commercial advertisements became more common. McGovern chose still longer programs consisting of his addresses on Vietnam and the issue of corruption. Semidocumentary formats, such as a candidate's discussing issues with ordinary citizens, were used as well. McGovern was filmed interacting with workers and owners of small businesses, and Nixon's trips to China and the Soviet Union were dramatized for television viewers.

In 1976 President Ford employed the medium more imaginatively than did Carter. The president held an informal television interview, for example, with television personality and former baseball player Joe Garagiola, who tossed him some "gopher-ball" questions: "How many foreign leaders have you met with, Mr. President?" to which Ford modestly replied, "One hundred and twenty-four, Joe." In the last stages of the campaign, the Ford forces also broadcast short television interviews with voters in Georgia who described Carter as "wishy-washy." Carter concentrated on short commercials in which he looked directly into the camera and talked about various issues, so as to counteract Ford's portrayal of him and to present himself as a strong, positive leader with specific programs.

During the 1980 campaign the television advertisements varied in length from thirty seconds to thirty minutes, but most were short spot messages designed to reach peak audiences. The Carter television commercials appeared in three separate stages: the first showed the candidate being presidential, meeting with foreign dignitaries and working late at night in the Oval Office; the second consisted of interviews with people "in the street" saying that Reagan "scared" them; the third showed Carter being praised by prominent party figures, such as Lady Bird Johnson and Edward Kennedy, and by rank-and-file Democrats--a farmer, a steelworker, and a worker in a rubber factory. Most of the Reagan television advertisements featured the candidate himself, whom the Republicans considered to be a superb communicator, looking straight into the camera. They stressed three themes: Reagan's record as governor of California; his stand on issues, especially the economy; and a recitation of the record of President Carter, illustrated with graphs of rising consumer prices.

In 1984 the Republicans aired a nostalgic, half-hour film of President Reagan riding his horse, walking on a hilltop with Nancy, speaking at the Normandy beaches, and taking the oath of office. Most of the Republican commercials, however, were thirty-second ones. The most famous, "It's morning again in America," showed the sun shining on San Francisco Bay, people hurrying to and from work, and a bride and groom kissing at a wedding while a mellifluous voice asked, "Why would we ever want to go back to where we were less than four short years ago?" The Democrats relied entirely on thirty-second spot commercials. One showed a roller coaster climbing its tracks (suggesting what will happen tomorrow as a result of record U.S. deficits), with a voice intoning, "If you're thinking of voting for Ronald Reagan in 1984, think of what will happen in 1985." Another, positive commercial pictured a warm, dynamic Walter Mondale talking to a group of students, urging them to "stretch their minds" and to live their dreams, telling them he wanted to help them be what they wanted to be.

In four elections, televised debates between presidential candidates became the most important communication source of the campaign.[21] The first occurred in 1960 between Richard Nixon, at that time Eisenhower's vice president, and Sen. John Kennedy. In the first of four debates, Nixon's somewhat uncertain manner and his physical appearance (he had not fully recovered from a recent illness and television accentuated his heavy beard) was contrasted with Kennedy's confident demeanor and bright, alert image (he wore a blue shirt and dark suit that showed up well against the television studio background rather than fading into it as Nixon's light-colored clothes did). Also, unlike Nixon, Kennedy had prepared thoroughly for the debates. As a result, viewers perceived a victory for the young Massachusetts senator.[22] Contributing to that perception was that people had not expected Kennedy to best Nixon, who had gained political prominence in part because of his debating skills in previous campaigns. From that point on, Kennedy's campaign assumed more enthusiasm, and the senator himself credited the debate for his eventual close victory over the vice president.

In 1976, presidential debates again played a major part in the campaign. In this case it was the second of those debates between President Ford and Jimmy Carter that proved crucial. In that debate, Ford stated that he did not consider countries of Eastern Europe (in particular, Yugoslavia, Romania, and Poland) to be under Soviet domination. To make matters worse, the president refused to change his answer even after the startled questioner (a newspaper reporter) gave him the opportunity to do so; in fact, it was not until several days after the debate that the president's staff finally persuaded him to retract his statement. Many political observers considered that gaffe to be the turning point of the contest, the one that ended the dramatic decline in public support for Carter (and the increased support for Ford) that had characterized the previous month of the campaign.

In 1980 the presidential debates became more complicated. The sponsors of the debate, the League of Women Voters, originally extended an invitation to debate not only to President Carter and Ronald Reagan but also to independent candidate John Anderson, whose standing in the public opinion polls exceeded the 15-percent cutoff point established by the League. Carter refused to participate on the grounds that the debate would legitimize the Anderson candidacy, which he asserted was strictly a "creation of the media." In contrast, Reagan, who perceived that Anderson would draw more votes away from Carter than from himself, accepted the League's invitation and criticized Carter for refusing to debate.

Ultimately, just a week before election day (when Anderson's public support had fallen below 15 percent), a single debate was held between the two major party candidates. Although both men looked and handled themselves well, and neither made a serious mistake, most observers concluded that Reagan won the debate on style rather than substance. Carter aides congratulated themselves that the president had kept the focus of the debate on Reagan rather than on his own presidential record, but the tactic apparently backfired. On the one hand, many viewers thought Carter was too aggressive in his accusations; on the other, they felt reassured by Reagan's responses and were convinced that he would not be a trigger-happy president if elected to the office.[23]

In 1984 the Mondale forces requested six separate presidential debates and a format in which the candidates could ask each other questions. The Reagan organization refused that request, and the sides ultimately agreed to two debates between Mondale and Reagan and one between the vice-presidential candidates, Bush and Ferraro. In all three, members of the media would ask the questions. The first presidential debate turned out to be a clear victory for the challenger, Mondale, who projected himself as calm, bright, and confident, while the president appeared confused, inarticulate, and in his summation, to have lost his train of thought altogether. When the president at one point repeated the line from his 1980 debate with Carter "there you go again," Mondale turned pointedly to Reagan and asked, "Remember the last time you said that?" and then answered the question himself: "You said it when President Carter said you were going to cut Medicare . . . and what did you do right after the election? You went out and tried to cut $20 billion out of Medicare." The debate sent shock waves through the Republican camp not only because the media and most observers (even Reagan supporters) agreed that the president had been defeated decisively, but also because the debate raised the issue of whether his age had slowed him down and made him incapable of handling the demands of the office for the next four years. The second debate, however, ended with a far different result: Reagan prevailed on style, appearing more relaxed and coherent (although he again rambled in his closing remarks). Most important, the president defused the age issue when, in response to a question on the matter, he replied that he did not intend "to exploit my opponent's youth and inexperience," a clever retort that drew a broad smile even from Mondale.

Besides political commercials and debates, a third source of communication in presidential campaigns is the coverage provided by representatives of the mass media themselves, both the broadcast media (television and radio) and print media (newspapers and magazines). These representatives are not nearly as important in general election campaigns, however, as they are in the nomination stage. By the time of the fall election, the campaign is much more structured. The contest essentially is down to two candidates, who by then are fairly well known to the electorate; in addition, the voters at this stage associate the candidates with their respective parties and evaluate them on that basis. Moreover, the candidates have more money to spend on campaign communications than they did in the nomination process; and debates, if they are held, are more focused (typically between only two candidates) and reach a wider audience than any that occurred in the nomination campaign.

The media's coverage of the election campaign is similar to that in the nomination stage. Reporters and commentators pay great attention to the election "game," that is, which party candidate is leading in the public opinion polls and by how much, and to the "hoopla"—campaign rallies and the like. The media also tend to focus on "campaign issues" rather than policy issues, such as Jimmy Carter's remark in the 1976 campaign that he "lusted after women in his heart" and Ford's comment about Eastern Europe. In 1980 the media played up Jimmy Carter's personal attacks on Ronald Reagan and on Reagan's contention that the literal, biblical interpretation of creation should be taught equally with the theory of evolution. In 1984 the media zeroed in on the financial affairs of Geraldine Ferraro and her husband.

Patterson's study of the 1976 election contest does indicate, however, that the voters became more aware of the candidates' positions on policy issues as the campaign progressed.[24] He attributes some of that increase to their familiarity with the policy tendencies of the Democratic and Republican parties. His analysis also shows that newspaper coverage of policy issues increased voters' awareness of them, particularly for voters who previously had not been highly interested in policy issues. In contrast, the short, superficial coverage of the issues by network news did not raise voters' awareness of the issues. More recent campaign studies, however, do not show the superiority of the print media. In their analysis of the 1980 campaign, Robinson and Sheehan conclude that the broadcast networks covered the issues at least as well as the wire services.[25] Moreover, Patterson and Davis found in their study of the 1984 campaign that only 4 of 114 newspaper articles they analyzed mentioned Mondale's charge that Reagan's tax cuts benefited the rich, and none mentioned Mondale's progressive tax plan.[26]

Thus, despite the dominance of television in recent presidential contests, the other media continue to play a role in campaigns. Newspapers not only cover the issues in more detail than television but also are free to endorse candidates.[27] The print media are also available for advertisements stressing visual effects. In 1960 the Democrats used pictures of John Kennedy and his attractive wife, Jacqueline, in many of their promotions. In 1976 the Republicans printed full-page advertisements comparing the cover of *Newsweek* magazine that featured President Ford with the cover of *Playboy* magazine that carried the controversial interview with Carter (in which he confessed that he "lusted after women in his heart").

Radio also plays a role in presidential campaigns. It is less expensive than television and can be used in ways that television cannot, such as broadcasting to commuting drivers, as President Ford did in a series of early morning chats during the 1976 campaign. There is also the distinct possibility that a particular candidate will come across better on radio, a reason suggested for President Nixon's using the medium more often than television for his speeches during the 1972 campaign. Moreover, some radio networks, such as National Public Radio, cover presidential campaigns in much greater depth than does television.

The formats available in the various media therefore make it possible for candidates to emphasize different types of appeals and to reach disparate groups. Nimmo distinguishes between two major types of audiences.[28] The first consists of the politically concerned and interested, who use the print media as well as television and radio to obtain information on presidential campaigns. The second comprises less politically involved voters who must be reached through television and sometimes through radio, particularly by means of spot announcements, such as those used by Richard Nixon during his 1968 campaign.

Campaign Organization and Workers

Although the mass media reach more people in the general election campaign than in the nomination contest (more money is spent in a shorter period of time, and some voters become politically interested only after the parties nominate their respective candidates), not everyone personally follows the election campaign, especially in print and on the radio. These voters depend on those who do follow it to pass along information, such as the candidates' stands on the issues. (Of course, the transmitters often alter the messages in keeping with their own views and biases.) Beyond that, personal contacts are particularly important in persuading many people to make the most basic political decision: whether or not to vote at all. Sometimes citizens' apathy can be overcome only by the dogged determination of persons who see that others register to vote and have transportation to the polls.

Presidential candidates typically start the general election campaign with a core of people who, in effect, constitute their personal organization. If there has been a spirited nomination battle, the principal organizers of the campaign shift their attention to the general election. John Kennedy put his brother Robert in charge of his 1960 campaign against Richard Nixon, and Hamilton Jordan continued as the head of Jimmy Carter's 1976 fall campaign. Others who worked for the candidate in the primary and caucus-convention states also usually are available for the election campaign. Incumbent presidents frequently assign key members of their administration to work on the fall campaign. In 1972 Richard Nixon initially put his attorney general, John Mitchell, in charge of the Committee to Reelect the President and transferred other persons in the White House office to assignments on the committee. Three important figures in the Carter administration, Robert Strauss, Hamilton Jordan, and Gerald Rafshoon, played significant roles in the 1980 campaign.

Because the electorate for the general campaign is so much broader than the selectorate, which participates in the nomination phase, presidential candidates must increase their number of supporters in the fall to include people who had not been involved previously. One potential source of new recruits is political rivals who had sought the nomination themselves. In 1972 George McGovern asked Hubert Humphrey to campaign for him; Humphrey did so out of personal friendship and party loyalty. In 1984 both Gary Hart and Jesse Jackson worked hard on Mondale's behalf in the fall campaign. In 1976 Ford and Reagan supporters cochaired the general election campaign in many states.[29] In many instances, however, personal loyalties and commitments to issues are so strong that it is not possible to recruit those who supported the other candidates for the nomination. In 1968 the Humphrey organization was not able to persuade many of Eugene McCarthy's supporters to work in the general election campaign after McCarthy lost the presidential nomination. In 1980 many people who backed Edward Kennedy's unsuccessful bid for the Democratic nomination did not work for President Carter in the fall campaign; nor in 1984 did many of Gary Hart's supporters campaign for Mondale.

Persons associated with the regular party organization are another potential source of campaign workers. Termed "organizational loyalists" by John Kessel, these are the people who owe their allegiance to the party instead of a particular presidential candidate or set of political issues.[30] Because of such loyalties, they are often willing to work in the fall campaign for whichever candidate wins their party's nomination, no matter what their personal feelings about the nominee may be. At the same time, because they are pragmatic and not ideological, party loyalists may not work hard for a presidential candidate who they think is a loser and who will hurt the candidacies of party representatives seeking other political offices. Many Republicans took this attitude toward Goldwater in 1964, as did some Democratic leaders toward Humphrey in 1968, McGovern in 1972, and Mondale in 1984.

State and local political parties are another potential source of workers for the presidential general election campaign. For several reasons, however, problems traditionally have arisen in persuading these organizations to work for the presidential candidates. First, state and local races are more important than the presidential contest to local leaders, particularly those in patronage positions. Second, national, state, and local organizations compete for the same resources, such as visits by candidates and financial donations. Finally, the campaign finance legislation passed in the early 1970s, providing public funds for presidential campaigns, prohibited state and local parties from spending money on such campaigns.

The 1979 amendment to the campaign finance legislation, however, permitted state and local party organizations to spend money in presidential campaigns for any purpose except campaign advertising and hiring outside personnel. This legislation enabled both parties in 1980 to develop grass-roots support for their presidential campaigns, although the Republicans clearly outdid the Democrats. Early in the fall campaign Reagan met with Republican members of Congress on the steps of the Capitol to symbolize cooperation among all elements of the party in electing Republicans to public office. As election day approached, the GOP stated that it had half a million Reagan volunteers ringing doorbells and another 400,000 staffing telephone banks on his behalf.

Democratic presidential candidates have generally benefited from another major source of campaign workers: those provided by organized labor. In 1968 the AFL-CIO (American Federation of Labor and Congress of Industrial Organizations) said it had registered 4.6 million voters, printed and distributed more than 100 million pamphlets, operated telephone banks in 638 localities, sent out 70,000 house-to-house canvassers, and provided almost 100,000 volunteers on election day to transport people to the polls.[31] This effort was extended on Hubert Humphrey's behalf and is credited with winning the votes of a large number of workers who initially planned to vote for George Wallace.

In contrast, the antipathy of George Meany and other AFL-CIO leaders toward George McGovern caused the organization to remain neutral in the 1972 presidential race and to concentrate its efforts instead toward helping Democrats win House seats and state and local offices. In 1976 the AFL-CIO returned to its traditional policy of supporting

Democratic presidential candidates and played an important role in registering its members and their families and in transporting them to the polls to vote for Jimmy Carter. In 1980, although some of its principal leaders backed Senator Kennedy in the Democratic nomination struggle, labor generally did support President Carter; the National Education Association was especially active on his behalf. In 1984, except for the Teamsters, who backed Reagan, labor unions were united on behalf of Walter Mondale.

One distinctive feature of the 1984 campaign was the extent to which both political parties sought to register new voters. Initially, observers thought that the Democrats would benefit most from this effort by registering traditionally low-voting groups such as blacks, Hispanics, and the poor. Their registration effort ran into difficulties, however, because of rivalries among organizations attempting to register the same people and the reluctance of some political organizations to add new voters who would later share in deciding which candidates would prevail in Democratic primary contests for various offices. Moreover, the Republican party launched an all-out drive of its own to counteract the rival party's effort. Republicans registered a large number of white southerners, with the assistance of fundamentalist ministers, and selected key states, such as California, Texas, and Florida, for special registration drives.

Campaign Finance

Since 1976, campaign reform legislation has significantly influenced general election campaigns. In 1976 both Ford and Carter accepted federal funds ($21.8 million each that year) and were therefore restricted to that figure for the entire campaign (plus another $3.2 million that each national committee could spend on behalf of its presidential candidate). As a result, both sides had to conduct more restricted campaigns than they did in 1972, when the Republicans spent $61 million and the Democrats $30 million. The public subsidy provided equally to both candidates meant that Ford had to forgo the traditional Republican advantage in campaign funds. As the incumbent president, however, he received a great deal of free publicity, and his Rose Garden strategy enabled him to reserve his financial resources for the last ten days of the campaign, in which he spent $4 million on television and radio broadcasting, primarily in airing the television commercials with Joe Garagiola. All told, both candidates spent about half of their total campaign outlay on the mass media, particularly television, and therefore had limited funds available for organizing their grass-roots campaigns. Largely missing from the 1976 contest were fund-raising activities and the buttons, bumper stickers, and yard signs, used extensively in previous elections (recall that under the law then in effect state and local parties could not assist the presidential campaign by spending money for such purposes).

The 1980 campaign brought new developments in campaign finance. The two major party candidates accepted public financing, and each spent about $18 million of the $29.4 million in federal funds on the mass media, which again meant that they had limited funds available for grass-roots activities. In 1980, however, the law permitted state and local parties to make expenditures for such activities. Figures provided by the Federal Election Commission show that Republican state and local committees spent $15 million on grass-roots efforts on Reagan's behalf compared with $5 million spent by Democratic organizations for Carter.

Also of increased importance in the 1980 campaign were the actions of independent groups in support of Reagan. In the summer of 1980 several organizations announced plans to spend up to $70 million on media efforts for the Republican candidate. A citizens' interest group, Common Cause, together with the Federal Election Commission and the Carter-Mondale Presidential Committee, legally challenged such expenditures on the grounds that the groups were not truly autonomous since some of their leaders had been closely associated with Reagan in past political campaigns. Although these challenges were unsuccessful, they did impede the fund-raising efforts of the independent groups and forced them to cut back on their original plans. Eventually, independent organizations spent approximately $10.6 million on Reagan's behalf. Although much less than originally anticipated, these expenditures were nonetheless significant: independent groups were estimated to have spent only $28,000 for President Carter, about one-quarter of 1 percent of the amount spent for Reagan.[32]

In 1984 both presidential candidates again spent a major portion of their federal funds ($40.4 million plus $6.9 million for the national committee) on the mass media. Both parties also expended considerable sums of money on voter registration efforts. The Republicans funneled much more money to state parties to assist in the campaign than the Democrats did.

Both the rules of the game and the campaign strategies and resources developed by the opposing candidates shape the outcome of presidential campaigns. The campaign, however, is only one influence on the way people vote. Chapter 4 examines other influences, as well as patterns of voting in presidential elections.

Notes

1. Max Farrand, *The Framing of the Constitution of the United States* (New Haven: Yale University Press, 1913), 160.
2. Neal Peirce, *The People's President: The Electoral College in American History and the Direct-Vote Alternative* (New York: Simon and Schuster, 1968), 430.
3. Lucius Wilmerding, *The Electoral College* (New Brunswick, N.J.: Rutgers University Press, 1958), chap. 8.
4. John Roche, "The Founding Fathers: A Reform Caucus in Action," *American Political Science Review* (December 1961): 811.
5. Lawrence Longley, "Minorities and the 1980 Electoral College" (Paper delivered at the annual meeting of the American Political Science Association, Washington, D.C., August 28-31, 1980).
6. The 270 electoral votes constitute a majority of the total number of 538. The number 538 is the total of 435 electoral votes representing members of the House of Representatives, 100 representing the senators from the fifty states, and 3 representing the District of Columbia.
7. Wallace, however, may have affected the results of the Truman-Dewey contest in some states; Wallace's winning 8 percent of the popular vote in New York State probably drained enough votes away from Truman to allow Dewey to defeat him by about 1 percent of the popular vote.
8. Although presidential candidates are free to refuse public funds, none has done so, perhaps because of the difficulty of raising money under the limitations on contributions from individuals and political action committees. Candidates may also think that the American public favors the use of public rather than private funds in the presidential general election.
9. Although campaign activities are carried in the national media, local media give special publicity to the candidate and thus affect the immediate audience. Moreover, some voters are flattered by the fact that a candidate takes the time and effort to come to their locality to campaign.
10. Lewis Chester, Godfrey Hodgson, and Bruce Page, *The American Melodrama: The Presidential Campaign of 1968* (New York: Viking, 1969), 620.
11. Presidential candidates sometimes, however, venture into states thought to belong politically to their opponents. In 1976 Jimmy Carter made some trips into normally Republican areas to put Ford on the defensive, therefore forcing him to spend time and money in states he expected to carry (Martin Schram, *Running for President 1976: The Carter Campaign* [New York: Stein and Day, 1977], 247). Carter in 1980 and Mondale in 1984 also visited California, in part to require Ronald Reagan to use some resources to protect his home state.
12. John Kessel reports the comment made during the 1972 campaign that "McGovern could not carry the South with Robert E. Lee as his running-mate and Bear Bryant as his campaign manager" (John Kessel, "Strategy for November," in *Choosing the President,* ed. James D. Barber [Englewood Cliffs, N.J.: Prentice-Hall, 1974], 109).
13. This carefully thought-out plan is to be contrasted with the pledge Richard Nixon made at the 1960 Republican national convention to visit all fifty states personally. In the closing days of the campaign, Nixon took precious time to fly to Alaska, which he had not previously visited, while his opponent,

John Kennedy, was barnstorming through heavily populated Illinois, New Jersey, New York, and the New England states.

14. Thomas Cronin, "The Presidential Election of 1984," in *Election 84: Landslide without a Mandate,* ed. Ellis Sandoz and Cecil Crabb, Jr. (New York: Mentor, 1985), 49.

15. Timothy Crouse, *The Boys on the Bus* (New York: Ballentine Books, 1972), 257.

16. One of the interesting features of the 1980 campaign was that President Carter did *not* use Vice President Mondale much in that way; instead, the president launched frequent personal attacks on Ronald Reagan himself while for the most part Mondale played the role of the "happy warrior" in the campaign.

17. In 1980 the Republicans handled the potential problem of an even older Ronald Reagan, who was almost seventy at the time of the fall campaign, in a very different way: he was depicted as an unusually vigorous man for one his age. This image was helped considerably by Reagan's full head of hair, as contrasted to Eisenhower's bald pate.

18. A variant of this problem occurred in 1984 for Walter Mondale. Although he was not the incumbent vice president, he did hold that office from 1977 to 1981 under Carter and was associated with the policies of that administration, some of which he did not agree with (placing an embargo on grain shipments to the Soviet Union, for example).

19. One political scientist calls "position issues" those that "involve advocacy of governmental action from a set of alternatives," in contrast to "valence issues," which "merely involve linking of the parties with some condition that is positively or negatively valued by the electorate" (Donald Stokes, "Special Models of Party Competition," in *Elections in the Political Order,* ed. Angus Campbell, Philip Converse, Warren Miller, and Donald Stokes [New York: Wiley, 1966], 170-171).

20. Marshall McLuhan, *Understanding Media: The Extensions of Man* (New York: McGraw-Hill, 1964), chap. 1.

21. A problem in holding presidential debates is a provision of the Federal Communications Act of 1934 requiring the networks to provide equal time to *all* candidates, including those of minor parties. In 1960 Congress temporarily suspended the provisions of the act to allow the Nixon-Kennedy debates. In 1976, 1980, and 1984 the debates were sponsored and paid for by the League of Women Voters. The networks supposedly covered them as "news events," a legal fiction that was exposed when the first Carter-Ford debate in 1976 was interrupted for twenty-eight minutes until an audio failure could be repaired.

22. This was especially true of people who watched the first Nixon-Kennedy debate on television. Those who heard that same debate on the radio, however, thought the two candidates came out about equally (Theodore White, *The Making of the President, 1960* [New York: Pocket Books, 1961], 348).

23. In addition, Albert Hunt suggests that Reagan convinced many viewers of the debate that he was sufficiently smart to go head-to-head with the president and not crumble. President Carter, however, did not meet the greater expectations the viewers had of his debate performance, namely, that he explain why things had not gone very well in the previous four years and how he would do better in a second term (Albert Hunt, "The Campaign and the

Issues," in *The American Elections of 1980,* ed. Austin Ranney [Washington, D.C.: American Enterprise Institute, 1981], 170-171).

24. Thomas Patterson, *The Mass Media Election: How Americans Choose Their President* (New York: Praeger, 1980), chap. 13.

25. Michael Robinson and Margaret Sheehan, *Over the Wire and on TV: CBS and UPI in Campaign '80* (New York: Russell Sage Foundation, 1983), 166.

26. Thomas Patterson and Richard Davis, "The Media Campaign: Struggle for the Agenda," in *The Elections of 1984,* ed. Michael Nelson (Washington, D.C.: CQ Press, 1985), 116.

27. Over the years endorsements have clearly favored the Republican candidate, except in 1964, when the press favored Johnson over Goldwater. As a group, newspaper owners and editors, who decide on endorsements, tend to be conservative, possibly because much of their advertising revenue comes from large corporations. Political reporters, by contrast, are widely perceived to be liberal.

28. Dan Nimmo, *The Political Persuaders: The Techniques of Modern Political Campaigns* (Englewood Cliffs, N.J.: Prentice-Hall, 1970), 117-118.

29. Jonathan Moore and Janet Fraser, *Campaign for President: The Managers Look at 1976* (Cambridge, Mass.: Ballinger, 1977), 133.

30. John Kessel, "Strategy for November," in *Choosing the President,* ed. James D. Barber (Englewood Cliffs, N.J.: Prentice-Hall, 1974), 179.

31. Theodore White, *The Making of the President, 1968* (New York: Bantam, 1969), 453-454.

32. Herbert E. Alexander, *Financing the 1980 Election* (Lexington, Mass.: D.C. Heath, 1983), 387.

Selected Readings

Abramson, Paul R., John H. Aldrich, and David W. Rohde. *Change and Continuity in the 1980 Elections.* Washington, D.C.: CQ Press, 1982.

———. *Change and Continuity in the 1984 Elections.* Rev. ed. Washington, D.C.: CQ Press, 1987.

Chubb, John, and Paul Peterson. *The New Direction in American Politics.* Washington, D.C.: Brookings, 1985.

Nelson, Michael, ed. *The Elections of 1984.* Washington, D.C.: CQ Press, 1985.

Ranney, Austin, ed. *The American Elections of 1980.* Washington, D.C.: American Enterprise Institute, 1981.

Robinson, Michael, and Margaret Sheehan. *Over the Wire and on TV: CBS and UPI in Campaign '80.* New York: Russell Sage Foundation, 1983.

Voting in Presidential Elections   4

The major purpose of presidential campaigns is to motivate people to take the time and effort to vote, and to vote for a particular candidate. Other factors also determine whether certain voters will cast a ballot in a presidential election. Moreover, for those who vote, the ultimate choice they make between candidates depends on their long-term political predispositions, such as political party loyalties and social group affiliations. Their choice also reflects their reactions to short-term forces, such as the particular candidates and issues involved in specific elections.

The first two sections of this chapter explore participation in presidential elections and the various factors that shape the voters' choice of candidates. The final section shifts to other important aspects of presidential elections—their effect on the political party system and on policy making in the United States.

Participation in Presidential Elections

As previously indicated, the Founders originally intended that the process of choosing the president and vice president would be restricted to members of the electoral college, the political elite of the day who were thought to have the intelligence and information to choose the best people to lead the country. The average person was considered incapable of making decisions of this kind. Important developments in U.S. politics, however, soon nullified such assumptions. As a result of the formation of the rival Federalist and Republican parties in the 1790s, electors began to vote the presidential preferences of the electorate instead of exercising their own judgment. Moreover, state legislatures that were granted power by the Constitution to determine how the electors should be chosen soon began vesting that right in the general electorate. In the process, the U.S.

presidential election system changed from an "elitist" to a "democratic" one.

This development was highly significant, but it left an important question unanswered. Who should be entitled to vote for the presidential electors? Making matters even less certain, the Constitution leaves that decision to the individual states, so that it is possible for some states to allow particular groups to vote for president while other states can prevent them from doing so. Consequently, it has sometimes been necessary for the federal government to take action to force all states to allow certain groups of people to participate in the selection of the chief executive.

An early state barrier to participation in presidential elections was the requirement that voters own *property*. Many legislatures took the position that only property owners would have enough of a "stake" in society to interest themselves in its political affairs. Some legislators also were concerned that the poor would sell their votes to unscrupulous politicians or, worse, use their votes to choose candidates who would proceed to redistribute the wealth of property owners. However, as more and more people acquired property and redistribution of wealth did not happen, state legislatures began to drop the property qualification for voting in presidential and other elections. By the early 1840s such qualifications had generally disappeared at the state level. Thus, the first major expansion of the presidential electorate took place without federal intervention—in contrast to other battles over the composition of the presidential electorate.

The most bitter franchise struggle involved the right of *blacks* to vote in all elections, including presidential contests. At the end of the Civil War, as part of a concerted program to bring liberated slaves into the mainstream of American life, the Fifteenth Amendment was passed. It stated that "the right of the citizens of the United States to vote shall not be denied or abridged by the United States or by any state, on account of race, color, or previous condition of servitude." For a short time, blacks did participate in presidential and other elections, but when federal troops withdrew from the South in the 1870s, a systematic disenfranchisement of blacks began. It took many forms, including physical violence; economic coercion; and legal devices, such as the exclusion of blacks from participating in primaries of the dominant Democratic party and the requirement to pay poll taxes (which also disenfranchised many poor whites) and to pass literacy tests (which were unfairly administered by election officials).

Unlike the property ownership voting qualification that the states themselves eliminated, it has been necessary for the federal government to take action on many occasions to force states to extend the right to vote to blacks. The earliest pressure came from the federal courts. In a 1915 decision, *Guinn v. United States,*[1] the Supreme Court invalidated the "grandfather" clause of the Oklahoma constitution, which exempted persons from a literacy test if their ancestors were entitled to vote in 1866; the Court viewed this as a deliberate (and not too subtle) attempt to avoid the Fifteenth Amendment's prohibition against denying certain citizens the right to vote. Ultimately, the Court in 1944 also outlawed "white" primaries, ruling in *Smith v. Allwright*[2] that a primary was a *public* function and not the business of a private organization—the Democratic party—as had been held in 1935 in *Grovey v. Townsend.*[3] Hence, "white" primaries were forbidden under the Fifteenth Amendment.

The two other branches of the national government lagged behind the courts in helping blacks to win the right to vote. Democratic presidents Franklin D. Roosevelt and Harry S Truman both favored their enfranchisement; but they were unsuccessful in persuading Congress, dominated by southern committee chairmen who could block legislation through the filibuster power, to move against poll taxes or even to enact an antilynching law. Not until 1957, during the Republican administration of Dwight D. Eisenhower, did Congress finally pass legislation giving the attorney general of the United States the right to seek judicial relief against persons violating the right of individuals to vote. Many southern election officials easily circumvented the law; they continued to harass blacks who tried to vote and destroyed records to cover up their actions. In 1960 Congress passed additional legislation that strengthened the enforcement of voting rights by authorizing courts to appoint voting referees to register persons deprived of the right to vote because of race or color and by making it a crime to destroy election records.

Building on these modest beginnings, Congress in the 1960s launched an attack against the disenfranchisement of blacks. It initiated the Twenty-fourth Amendment outlawing the use of the poll tax in presidential and congressional elections; the states ratified the amendment in early 1964.[4] The following year, Congress responded to President Lyndon B. Johnson's leadership by enacting the Voting Rights Act of 1965, which suspended literacy tests and authorized the appointment of federal examiners to supervise electoral procedures in areas using such tests where less than one-half the voting-age population was registered or had voted in 1964. The act subsequently was amended in 1970 to cover areas where a similar situation existed in November 1968. In 1975 the act was extended for seven years more, and its provisions were expanded to cover the voting rights of other minorities, including people of Spanish heritage, American Indians, Asian-Americans, and Alaskan natives. In 1982, after some initial difficulties,[5] the act was extended for twenty-five years with provisions requiring certain areas of the country to provide bilingual election materials until 1992.

The national government also has taken action to expand the electorate to include two other major groups: *women* and *young people*. Even though some states had acted on their own to enfranchise both groups, Congress ultimately decided to require all states to do so. In 1920 the states ratified the Nineteenth Amendment, which forbade either the United States or any one state from denying a U.S. citizen the right to vote "on account of sex." Young people won a major victory in the early 1970s. Congress first passed a law granting eighteen-year-olds the right to vote in national, state, and local elections. When the Supreme Court ruled that a national law could affect voting only in national elections, the Twenty-sixth Amendment was enacted to extend the right to state and local elections.

Congress has initiated other actions to expand the presidential electorate. The Twenty-third Amendment, ratified in 1961, grants residents of the District of Columbia the right to vote in presidential elections, a privilege they had been denied since the capital was located there in 1800. The 1970 act that lowered the voting age to eighteen also provides that people may vote in presidential elections if they have lived at their current residence for at least thirty days.

Thus, the number of people who are eligible to vote in presidential elections has increased greatly over the years. The right to vote and the actual exercise of that right are, however, two separate matters.

General Trends in Voter Turnout

One of the ironies of U.S. presidential elections in recent years is that as more and more citizens have acquired the right to vote, a smaller and smaller proportion of them have exercised that right. As Table 4-1 indicates, the estimated number of people of voting age has more than doubled since Franklin Roosevelt was first elected to office in 1932. After reaching a peak in 1960, however, the percentage of people who actually went to the polls declined in the next five presidential elections and rose only slightly in 1984. The most pronounced drop—over 5 percent—occurred between the 1968 and 1972 elections.

This recent decline in voter participation runs counter to some of the traditional theories of why people do not vote. Restrictive laws, particularly those pertaining to registration and voting, frequently are said to prevent citizens from going to the polls. Yet many states have eased such restrictions in recent years, and the Congress has facilitated voting in presidential elections for new residents, so that it generally was easier for a person to register and to vote for president in 1980 than it was in

Table 4-1 Participation of General Public in Presidential Elections, 1932-1984

Year	Estimated population of voting age (millions)	Number of votes cast (millions)	Percentage of vote cast
1932	75.8	39.7	52.4
1936	80.2	45.6	56.0
1940	84.7	49.9	58.9
1944	85.7	48.0	56.0
1948	95.6	48.8	51.1
1952	99.9	61.6	61.6
1956	104.5	62.0	59.3
1960	109.7	68.8	62.8
1964	114.1	70.6	61.9
1968	120.3	73.2	60.9
1972[a]	140.8	77.7	55.2
1976[a]	152.3	81.6	53.5
1980[a]	164.4	86.5	52.6
1984[a]	174.4	92.7	53.1

Source: *Statistical Abstract of the United States,* 1987, table no. 418 (Washington, D.C.: Government Printing Office, 1987).

[a] Elections in which persons eighteen to twenty years old were eligible to vote in all states.

1960. A person's lack of education also is often cited as a reason for not voting; however, the level of education of U.S. citizens was higher in 1980 than in 1960. The failure to vote frequently is linked to a lack of political information; however, because of increased use of the mass media, and particularly because of the televising of the Carter-Reagan debate in 1980, more Americans than ever (over 100 million tuned in to the debate) were made aware of the candidates and their views on public issues. Finally, close political races are supposed to stimulate people to get out and vote because they think their ballot might conceivably make a difference in the outcome. Pollsters forecast that the 1964 and 1972 elections would be landslides and that the 1968, 1976, and 1980 elections would be close contests, but a smaller percentage of people voted in 1968 than in 1964, and participation also declined in 1976 and 1980.[6]

It is possible to attribute some of the decline in voter turnout in recent years to the extension of the right to vote to eighteen-year-olds, which first took effect in the 1972 presidential election. Analyses of participation in that election by age group showed that eighteen- to twenty-year-olds did not vote as much (proportionately to their number) as did people twenty-one and over. (See Table 4-2.) Therefore, some of the overall 5 percent decline in voter turnout between 1968 and 1972 was caused by the addition of people to the potential electorate in the latter year who were less inclined to vote. This factor, however, does not help to explain the decline in participation between 1964 and 1968 and again in 1976 and 1980. Moreover, analyses of the 1972 election indicate that people twenty-one and over did not participate as much (proportionately) as they did in 1968.

Table 4-2 Participation of Various Groups in Presidential Elections, 1972-1984 (Percent)

| | Year | | | |
Group characteristic	1972	1976	1980	1984
Male	64.1	59.6	59.1	59.0
Female	62.0	58.8	59.4	60.8
White	64.5	60.9	60.9	61.4
Black	52.1	48.7	50.5	55.8
Age				
18-20 years old	48.3	38.0	35.7	36.7
21-24 years old	50.7	45.6	43.1	43.5
25-34 years old	59.7	55.4	54.6	54.5
35-44 years old	66.3	63.3	64.4	63.5
45-64 years old	70.8	68.7	69.3	69.8
65 and over	63.5	62.2	65.1	67.7
Residence				
Northeast	NA	59.5	58.5	59.7
Midwest	NA	65.1	65.8	65.7
South	55.4	54.9	55.6	56.8
West	NA	57.5	57.2	58.5
School year completed				
Grade 8 or less	47.4	44.1	42.6	42.9
Grade 9 to 12	52.0	47.2	45.6	44.4
Grade 12	65.4	59.4	58.9	58.7
College				
1-3 years	74.9	68.1	67.2	67.5
4 years or more	83.6	79.8	79.9	79.1

Note: Data are based on estimated population of voting age. The percentages are based on those *reporting* that they voted and are higher than those who actually voted. NA = Not available.

Source: *The Statistical Abstract of the United States*, 1987, table 420 (Washington, D.C.: Government Printing Office, 1987).

It is difficult to determine why voting has declined in presidential elections in recent years. Abramson, Aldrich, and Rohde, who analyze this decline in *reported* turnout in all presidential elections from 1952 through 1980, link it to two major factors.[7] The first is an erosion in the strength of political party identification of many Americans (the next section contains a discussion of that matter), which they feel results in less psychological involvement in politics. The second factor is a decline in a sense of political efficacy: over the years, fewer and fewer people have thought that public officials care about their opinions, and many have felt that as citizens they have little to say about what the government does. These attitudes, in turn, relate to public disaffection with the government's policies on issues such as race relations, Vietnam, and the Watergate scandals, as well as a general feeling that government has failed to solve the country's economic and social problems.

Group Differences in Voter Turnout

As shown in Table 4-2, participation in presidential elections varies among groups. Blacks and young people—two groups who participate the least—were formerly denied the franchise. One possible reason for this pattern is that some of the "newly" enfranchised may still be affected by public attitudes that originally denied them the right to vote. Nonwhites, especially older people who grew up in the South where they formerly could not vote, may feel that they are not able to make good choices. Some eighteen- to twenty-year-olds may also feel that they are too immature to exercise the right to vote intelligently. In all probability, however, the voting patterns of these two groups are attributable to other factors as well. Many blacks still have a limited education, which, as Table 4-2 shows, is linked to low voting participation. Many eighteen- to twenty-year-olds have not yet settled down and become involved in community affairs, another factor related to voting turnout. It is significant to note that women, another group that traditionally has had a comparatively low rate of participation, now vote more than men, a development probably linked to the increased level of education now achieved by women. (In recent years, women have begun to outnumber men among college students.)

Group differences in voter turnout are rooted in psychological feelings that affect all kinds of political participation, including voting. Well-educated people are more likely to be aware of political developments and their significance than poorly educated people. In addition, well-educated people tend to feel politically efficacious. They have a sense of confidence about the value of their opinions and believe that people in public office will listen to them; therefore, they think that what they do has an important effect on the political process. Poorly educated persons, however, are likely to feel that political officials do not care about them or their opinions. General attitudes about other people also affect voting behavior; those who trust people are more likely to cast their ballots than those whose cynicism and hostility toward others make them feel alienated.

The influence of a group is frequently important. Thus, if individuals belong to a business organization or labor union whose members talk much about political affairs, they may develop their own interests in such matters. If so, their political interests probably will lead them to make the effort to vote. Moreover, even if people are not interested in politics, they may feel that it is nevertheless their duty as a citizen to vote. This attitude is much more likely to exist in the upper and middle classes than in the lower class.

The reasons that prompt some people to vote and lead others to remain at home on election day are, indeed, varied; yet the factors that shape preferences between competing groups of presidential candidates are even more complex.

Voting Preferences in Presidential Elections

Long-term political dispositions that voters begin to acquire early in life, such as party affiliation and social group loyalties, affect how they vote in presidential elections. So do short-term forces, such as the particular candidates and issues involved in specific elections. Over the years, however, these individual factors have exerted varying degrees of influence in different elections.

Party Affiliation

Analyses of presidential elections in the 1950s by one group of researchers at the University of Michigan indicate that the single most important determinant of voting at that time was the party affiliation of the voter.[8] This general psychological attachment, shaped by family and social groups, tended to intensify with age. For the average person looking for guidance on how to vote amid the complexities of personalities, issues, and events of the 1950s, the party label of the candidates was the most important reference point. In this era—which voting analyst Philip Converse refers to as the "Steady State" period[9]—partisanship was also fairly constant. When asked, about 45 percent of Americans in 1952 and 1956 said they thought of themselves as Democrats; about 28 percent, as Republicans. When asked to classify themselves further as "strong" or "weak" partisans, both Republicans and Democrats tended to divide equally between those two categories. Independents in 1952 and 1956 averaged about 23 percent of the electorate.

In the mid- to late 1960s, however, partisan affiliation in the United States began to change. (See Table 4-3.) In 1964, party affiliation among the voters rose about 5 percent for the Democrats but fell about 3 percent for the Republicans; the independents' share of the electorate also declined slightly. Beginning with the 1968 election, the number of independents began to increase, primarily at the expense of the Democrats, until they constituted one-third of the electorate in 1972. Even those voters who stayed with the Democrats were more inclined than formerly to say they were weak rather than strong party members. Moreover, after 1968, more people identified themselves as independents than as Republicans.

Another indication of the declining importance of political party identification in presidential elections is the increase in recent years in the number of "switchers," that is, people who vote for one party's candidate in one presidential election and for another party's candidate in the following election. Analyses of presidential voting from 1940 to 1960 show that approximately one-eighth to one-fifth of the electorate switched from one election to the next.[10] From 1968 to 1980 the proportion ranged from one-fifth to one-third.[11] A similar phenomenon has occurred in split-ticket voting, that is, voting for candidates of more than one party in the same election. In 1952, some 13 percent of the Americans who voted cast a split ticket in presidential-House races; by 1972, 30 percent did. The number of split-ticket voters declined to 26 percent in 1976, rose to 35 percent in 1980, and declined to 25 percent in 1984.[12] Still more significant, even voters who identify with one of the

Table 4-3 Party Identification, 1952-1984 (Percent)

Party	1952	1956	1960	1964	1968	1972	1976	1980	1984
Strong Democrat	22	21	21	26	20	15	15	17	17
Weak Democrat	25	23	25	25	25	25	25	23	20
Total	47	44	46	51	45	40	40	40	37
Strong Republican	14	14	13	13	14	13	9	9	13
Weak Republican	13	15	14	11	10	10	14	14	15
Total	27	29	27	24	24	23	23	23	28
Independent	22	24	25	23	30	35	36	34	34

Source: The University of Michigan Center for Political Studies.

major parties have increasingly displayed partisan disloyalty by switching and ticket splitting.

Thus, independence from political parties, whether measured by voters' expressed attitudes toward the parties themselves or by reports of their actual behavior in the voting booth, has increased in recent years in the United States. This rise in independents is not, however, spread evenly across the voting population.[13] It has occurred primarily among young people, particularly those who entered the electorate in 1964 or later. New voters who came of age since that time are much more likely to be political independents than are voters of earlier political generations.

Independents in the United States not only have grown dramatically in numbers but also have changed in character. In the 1950s, independents tended to be less knowledgeable about political issues and candidates and to participate less in the political process than partisans.[14] Since the early 1960s, however, they have shown themselves to be just as knowledgeable about political matters as Democrats and Republicans.[15] Furthermore, although not as likely to vote as are party identifiers, independents do participate at least as much as partisans in other political activities, such as writing to political officials and voting on referendums. Thus, nonpartisanship, rather than general political disinterest, characterizes many of the younger independents, particularly those with a college education. A new type of independent seems to have joined the ranks of nonpartisans prevalent in the 1950s.

Observers of voting behavior have suggested several possible reasons for the decline in partisanship among U.S. voters. One is the decreased transfer of partisanship from one generation to the next; beginning in the late 1960s younger groups became less likely than earlier generations to retain their family partisan affiliation.[16] Two political "shock" periods, as Converse calls them, also weakened partisan loyalties.[17] The first, which began in 1965 and stemmed from the Vietnam War and racial unrest, affected voters of all ages, Democrats somewhat more than Republicans. The second, which began in 1972 and was precipitated by Watergate and the disclosure that led to Vice President Spiro Agnew's resignation, had a distinct impact on older Republicans.

As shown in Table 4-3, however, the decline in partisanship reached its peak in 1972. The proportion of independents did not change significantly in the three presidential elections after that. The trend away from party affiliation therefore appears to have stopped. Moreover, in the mid-1980s the number of voters identifying with the Republican party has increased while the number identifying with the Democratic party has decreased.

Social Groups and Social Class

Analysts of the presidential elections of 1940 and of 1948 found that a fairly close association existed between voters' social group membership and social status and their support for one of the two major parties.[18] Democrats received most of their support from southerners, blacks, Catholics, and people with limited education, lower incomes, and a working-class background. Republican candidates were supported by northerners, whites, Protestants, and people with more education, higher incomes, and a professional or business background.

Table 4-4 shows how various groups voted in presidential elections from 1952 through 1984. The support of many groups for their traditional party's candidates declined over the thirty-two-year period. Especially noticeable for the Republicans was their loss of votes from white-collar workers and Protestants. The most significant drop for the Democrats came in the southern vote in the 1968 and 1972 elections. The party regained this vote in 1976, however, when Jimmy Carter, of Georgia, headed the ticket (only to lose it again in 1980 and 1984). The only group that significantly increased its support for its traditional party candidate over the thirty-two-year period was nonwhites, who have been more firmly in the Democratic camp since 1964 than they were in 1952.

Table 4-4 also shows that the circumstances of particular elections can greatly alter group voting tendencies. In 1964, when the very conservative Barry Goldwater was the Republican standard-bearer, all the groups, including those that typically support the GOP (Grand Old Party), voted for the Democratic candidate, Lyndon Johnson. In 1972, when the very liberal George McGovern ran on the Democratic ticket, all the groups that usually sympathize with that party, except for nonwhites, voted for the Republican candidate, Richard Nixon. In 1984, when Walter Mondale, a traditional, New Deal Democrat, ran against the highly popular Republican president, Ronald Reagan, the Democrats won the overwhelming support only of nonwhites and, by a narrow margin, people with a grade school education and members of labor unions.

Table 4-4 also makes clear how much additional group support Reagan picked up in 1984 compared with 1980. In every category, a greater percentage of voters supported Reagan after four years as president than when he first ran for the office. The increases were particularly pronounced among voters under age thirty (19 percent), Catholics (14 percent), and males, professional and business people, and southerners (11 percent each).[19]

Party identification and group affiliation, therefore, have not meant as much in recent presidential voting as they once did. Other forces, such

Table 4-4 Group Voting Patterns in Presidential Elections, 1952-1984 (Percent)

	1952		1956		1960		1964	
	Stevenson	Eisenhower	Stevenson	Eisenhower	Kennedy	Nixon	Johnson	Goldwater
Group								
Sex								
male	47	53	45	55	52	48	60	40
female	42	58	39	61	49	51	62	38
Race								
white	43	57	41	59	49	51	59	41
nonwhite	79	21	61	39	68	32	94	6
Education								
college	34	66	31	69	39	61	52	48
high school	45	55	42	58	52	48	62	38
grade school	52	48	50	50	55	45	66	34
Occupation								
professional, business	36	64	32	68	42	58	54	46
white collar	40	60	37	63	48	52	57	43
manual	55	45	50	50	60	40	71	29
Age								
under 30	51	49	43	57	54	45	64	36
30-49	47	53	45	55	54	46	63	37
50 and older	39	61	39	61	46	54	59	41
Religion								
Protestant	37	63	37	63	38	62	55	45
Catholic	56	44	51	49	78	22	76	24
Region								
East	45	55	40	60	53	47	68	32
Midwest	42	58	41	59	48	52	61	39
South	51	49	49	51	51	49	52	48
West	42	58	43	57	49	51	60	40
Members of labor union families	61	39	57	43	65	35	73	27
National	44.6	55.4	42.2	57.8	50.1	49.9	61.3	38.7

Source: Excerpted from *Gallup Report,* November 1984, 8, 9.

as candidates, issues, events, and presidential performance are now more important in the political world of the American voter.

Table 4-4 (Continued)

	1968			1972		1976		1980			1984	
	Humphrey	Nixon	Wallace	McGovern	Nixon	Carter	Ford	Carter	Reagan	Anderson	Mondale	Reagan
	41	43	16	37	63	53	45	38	53	7	36	64
	45	43	12	38	62	48	51	44	49	6	45	55
	38	47	15	32	68	46	52	36	56	7	34	66
	85	12	3	87	13	85	15	86	10	2	87	13
	37	54	9	37	63	42	55	35	53	10	39	61
	42	43	15	34	66	54	46	43	51	5	43	57
	52	33	15	49	51	58	41	54	42	3	51	49
	34	56	10	31	69	42	56	33	55	10	34	66
	41	47	12	36	64	50	48	40	51	9	47	53
	50	35	15	43	57	58	41	48	46	5	46	54
	47	38	15	48	52	53	45	47	41	11	40	60
	44	41	15	33	67	48	49	38	52	8	40	60
	41	47	12	36	64	52	48	41	54	4	41	59
	35	49	16	30	70	46	53	39	54	6	39	61
	59	33	8	48	52	57	42	46	47	6	39	61
	50	43	7	42	58	51	47	43	47	9	46	54
	44	47	9	40	60	48	50	41	51	7	42	58
	31	36	33	29	71	54	45	44	52	3	37	63
	44	49	7	41	59	46	51	35	54	9	40	60
	56	29	15	46	54	63	36	50	43	5	52	48
	43.0	43.4	13.6	38	62	50	48	41	51	7	41	59

Candidates

The precise influence of candidates on the outcome of elections is difficult to determine. It is much easier for observers of the process to focus on the specific qualities of a particular candidate, such as Eisenhower's personal warmth, Kennedy's youth and Catholicism, and Johnson's expansive style, than it is to compare candidates systematically over a series of elections.[20]

Recognizing these limitations, scholars nonetheless have made some overall comparisons of voters' reactions to candidates from 1952 through 1980. Each presidential election year, the University of Michigan Center for Political Studies asked people whether there was anything about each of the major candidates that would make them want to vote for or against that person. The total number of favorable and unfavorable comments were then tabulated for each candidate; the more numerous the favorable comments about a candidate, the more positive the score. The overall scores, positive and negative, of the Republican and Democratic party candidates were compared with one another to determine the relative appeal of the nominees in each election year. (See Figure 4-1.)

Two significant findings are revealed in Figure 4-1. One is the variability of voters' attitudes toward the candidates over the course of the eight presidential elections from 1952 to 1980. The differences in candidate appeal were much less pronounced in 1952, 1960, 1968, 1976, and 1980 than they were in 1956, 1964, and 1972. The second finding is that except for 1964 and 1976, voters evaluated the Republican candidate more favorably than the Democratic candidate. Although it is not noteworthy that Dwight Eisenhower was more popular than Adlai Stevenson in 1956 and that Richard Nixon received a more favorable rating from the voters than George McGovern in 1972, it is somewhat surprising to find that Nixon was evaluated higher by the voters than John F. Kennedy in 1960.

Herbert Asher has suggested possible reasons Republican candidates usually have been more popular than their Democratic opponents since 1952.[21] One is that the Democratic party draws support from a broader variety of groups than the Republican party does, so it is more difficult for the Democratic nominee to please all the elements of the party. Another possible explanation is that since Republicans have been the minority party, they have to be particularly careful to nominate very attractive candidates. Finally, the nature of the times has favored Republican candidates. In 1952 and 1968 the incumbent Democratic party was faced with defending the Korean and Vietnam wars; such hostilities were either over or virtually over when the Republicans were the incumbent party in 1956 and 1972. In 1980 the Democratic administration was beset with the Iranian crisis and also with high inflation caused by rising oil prices.

Figure 4-1 Appeal of Democratic and Republican Candidates for President, 1952-1980

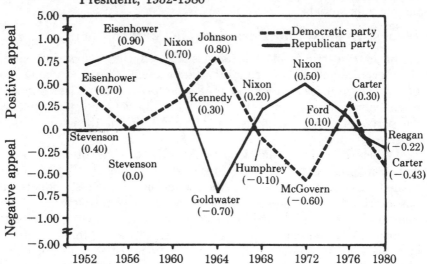

Sources: Arthur Miller and Warren Miller, "Partisanship and Performance: Rational Choice in the 1976 Presidential Election" (Paper delivered at the annual meeting of the American Political Science Association, Washington, D.C., September 1-4, 1977), 90. The 1980 data are from Arthur Miller, "Policy and Performance Voting in the 1980 Election" (Paper delivered at the annual meeting of the American Political Science Association, New York, September 3-6, 1981), Figure 1. (All data are based on the American National Election Studies conducted by the Center for Political Studies, University of Michigan.)

Note: The numbers 5.00 and −5.00 are the greatest possible positive and negative scores, because 5 is the maximum number of comments that were tabulated over the election series. The number shown with each candidate's name is his composite score.

The survey by the Michigan Center for Political Studies suggests that voters' attitudes toward candidates stem from diverse sources: the party affiliations of the candidates, their stands on issues, voters percep- tions of how the candidates managed or would manage the government, and their personality and character traits. In order to focus more particularly on personal qualities alone, in the 1984 study the Michigan group asked respondents to evaluate Reagan and Mondale on twelve specific traits, which they combined into four summary measures: (1) leadership (commands respect, is inspiring, provides strong leadership); (2) competence (is hard-working, intelligent, and knowledgeable); (3) integrity (is decent, is moral, sets a good example); and (4) empathy (is compassionate, is kind, "really cares about people like you"). In contrast to some expectations, Reagan was favored over Mondale on only two of those four measures, leadership and integrity (Mondale prevailed on competence and empathy); and only on leadership was the president's margin substantial.[22]

Issues, Events, and Presidential Performance

Michigan researchers in the 1950s suggested that issues influence a voter's choice only if three conditions are present.[23] First, the voter must be aware that an issue or a number of issues exist. Second, issues must be of some personal concern to the voter. Third, the voter must perceive that one party better represents his or her own thinking on the issues than the other party does.

When these three conditions were applied to U.S. voters in the 1952 and 1956 presidential elections, researchers found that these criteria existed for relatively few voters. About one-third of the respondents were not aware of *any* of the sixteen principal issues about which they were questioned. Even the two-thirds who were aware of one or more issues frequently were not personally concerned about them. Finally, a number of those who were aware and concerned about issues were not able to perceive differences between the two parties' positions on them. The conclusion of the analysis was that issues *potentially* determined the choice of, at the most, only one-third of the electorate. (The proportion who *actually* voted as they did because of issues could have been, and probably was, even less.)

Studies of political attitudes in the 1960s[24] and 1970s[25] show that issues had become more important to voters. In this period the number and types of issues of which voters were aware increased. Voters during the Eisenhower years had exhibited some interest in traditional domestic matters (welfare, labor-management relationships) and in a few foreign policy issues (the threat of communism, the atomic bomb); beginning with the 1964 election, however, voters' interests broadened to include concerns such as civil rights and Vietnam. Vietnam in particular remained a prominent consideration in the 1968 and 1972 contests and was joined by new matters such as crime, disorder, and juvenile delinquency (sometimes referred to collectively along with race problems as the "social issue").

The connection between voters' own attitudes on issues and their perceptions of where the parties stand on them has grown closer since the early 1960s. Gerald Pomper's analysis of voters' attitudes on issues from 1956 through 1972 shows that beginning with the 1964 presidential election, attitudes became more aligned with partisan identification.[26] Democrats were more likely to express the "liberal" position on economic, civil rights, and foreign policy issues than were Republicans. Also, voters in the 1960s perceived more clearly than voters in the 1950s the differences between the general approaches the two parties take on issues. During this decade a consensus developed that the Democratic party takes a liberal stand, and the Republican party, a conservative one. With these developments, the potential for voting on the basis of issues has increased in recent years. Correlations of voters' attitudes on issues with the way they voted in presidential elections in the 1960s as compared with the 1950s also show that this potential for issue voting was converted into actuality.

Recent analyses also reveal a change in the way the American people think about politics. When voters in the 1950s were asked to indicate what they liked or disliked about the candidates and the parties, only about one in ten responded in ideological terms by linking his or her attitudes on such matters to political issues or by mentioning such general concepts as "liberal" or "conservative" to describe differences between candidates and parties. Far more people made references to group benefits—such as Democrats helping the worker, Republicans helping business—or to the nature of the times, linking Democrats to foreign wars and Republicans to economic downturns and depressions. More than one-fifth of the voters in the 1950s gave replies that had no issue content at all, such as "I just like Democrats better than Republicans" or "Ike's my man." In the 1960s and early 1970s, however, the number of "ideologues" increased considerably, to as much as one-third of the electorate in 1972, for example.[27] Particularly noticeable was a movement away from the perception of politics primarily from the vantage point of group benefits and toward a broader view of issues and general political ideas.

In addition to this broadening of the conceptualization of politics, voters increasingly related political issues to one another as liberal or conservative. Studies of the electorate in the 1950s showed that voters were inconsistent in this respect; that is, people who took the "liberal" position that government should take an active role in providing welfare for the needy did not necessarily think it should assume a similar role in encouraging racial integration in the schools.[28] Nor were voters' attitudes on either of these domestic matters related to their opinions on the foreign policy issue of what stand the U.S. government should take toward the threat of communism in the world. Beginning with the 1964 election, however, voters attitudes were more often correlated, showing consistency among domestic issues as well as between domestic and foreign issues.[29]

Many observers assumed that the decline in social unrest, produced by the U.S. involvement in Vietnam and the racial tensions of the late

1960s and early 1970s, would mean a return to a less ideological and issue-related presidential election in 1976. A study of that election by political scientists Arthur Miller and Warren Miller indicates, however, that this did not occur.[30] Using the same criteria that were used to discern the development of ideological thinking in the earlier period—voters' liberal and conservative attitudes on issues, their perceptions of party differences on such matters, and a correlation among their attitudes on issues—Miller and Miller concluded that ideological thinking declined only slightly between 1972 and 1976. Economic matters were much more important to the electorate in 1976 than social or cultural issues; Democrats were particularly concerned over the rise in unemployment before the election. Because many people believed that the Democratic party would do a better job than the Republican party in dealing with unemployment, and because Carter emphasized economic issues over noneconomic ones in his campaign, many voters distinguished between the two parties and their respective candidates on economic grounds. As Miller and Miller stated, the results of the 1976 election ultimately turned on "incumbent performance [Ford's] versus partisan ideology [Democratic]."

Analysis of the 1980 election shows that economic issues were again more important to the electorate that year than were social and cultural issues, with inflation being the most important concern for many voters. Arthur Miller attributes President Carter's defeat primarily to voter dissatisfaction with his performance in office, particularly his inability to deal with the economy and, to a lesser extent, with a perceived decline in U.S. prestige in the world.[31] Warren Miller, too, sees dissatisfaction with the incumbent's performance in office as an important element in his defeat but also believes that many people voted for Reagan because they agreed with his conservative policies.[32] Other analysts also conclude that dissatisfaction with Carter's performance in office and evaluations of the policy stands of the two major candidates were reasons for Reagan's victory, but dissatisfaction with Carter was somewhat more important than ideological considerations.[33]

The economy was again on the minds of the U.S. electorate in 1984 and was a major reason for President Reagan's overwhelming victory over Mondale. The voters were generally more satisfied with their family's financial situation and with national economic conditions than they were in 1980, and they credited President Reagan with bringing about those positive changes. In fact, there was an optimistic feeling about the general state of the nation, which again was attributed to the president's leadership. As in 1980, the performance of the incumbent significantly influenced the voting decisions of the electorate, but in 1984, the incumbent's performance was the primary reason for *retaining* rather than *removing* the president from office. Moreover, Mondale's vice presidency in the Carter administration allowed the electorate to compare the performance of the present administration with the previous one, rather than choosing between the incumbent and an unfamiliar and untested challenger.[34]

The electorate also evaluated the candidates' policy positions differently in the 1984 and the 1980 elections. In 1980, voters generally approved of Reagan's conservative policies, but in 1984, voters were actually closer to the liberal views of Mondale on desired policy *changes* than they were to the conservative views of the president (especially on cutting defense spending, increasing government aid to women, and avoiding involvement in Central America).[35] At the same time, the electorate was in general agreement with the *current* policies of the Reagan administration.[36] Between 1980 and 1984 it seems that the Reagan administration shifted government policies in the direction of increasing spending for defense and reducing domestic programs, and by 1984 the electorate had decided that the shift had gone far enough and should not be continued.

Many forces, therefore, influence voting behavior in presidential elections. Over the years the two major parties have developed different characteristics, and voters associate candidates with those characteristics. Democratic candidates have been favorably regarded for their party affiliation, their attitudes toward social groups, and their stands on domestic issues. In contrast, Republican ones have benefited from their positions on foreign policy issues, their party philosophy, their perceived ability to manage the government, and a generally favorable assessment of them as candidates.

Consequences of Presidential Elections

The most immediate and most obvious consequence of a presidential election is the voters' choice of a leader of the country and of the executive branch in particular for the succeeding term of office. As the following discussion indicates, however, presidential elections have broader political effects as well.

Effect on the Political Party System

Campbell and his associates have categorized presidential elections according to three clusters of electoral factors.[37] A *maintaining election* is one in which the long-term partisan orientation of the electorate keeps the traditional majority party in power (since 1932, the Democrats). The majority party candidate wins primarily because the people vote according to their traditional party loyalties. Short-term forces, such as candidates and issues, are present, but instead of determining which party wins, they contribute to the size of the majority party's victory. When they favor that party, as they did in 1964 when Goldwater was the Republican nominee, the vote margin separating the two major candidates is larger than usual. If short-term forces are in balance, as they were in 1948, the vote division approximates the proportion of voters who identify with the two parties.

A *deviating election* occurs when short-term forces benefit the minority party and override the long-term partisan preferences of the electorate. An especially appealing candidate or an outstanding issue, event, or type of presidential performance allows the minority party candidate to win with the support of some majority party members, independents, and a good share of new voters. The electorate does not, however, change its basic party preferences. Examples of deviating elections are those of 1952, 1956, 1968, and 1972: they were won by the Republican candidates, Eisenhower and Nixon, but the commitment of many voters to the majority party—the Democrats—was unaltered.[38]

An election that brings about major political change is a *realigning election*. These elections entail a major realignment of electoral support among blocs of voters who switch their traditional party affiliation. An unusually large number of new voters may also enter the electoral arena and cast their ballots disproportionately for one party's candidate. Unlike the deviating election, the effects of the realigning election persist in durable loyalties to the advantaged party. Political historians usually include five elections in the realigning category: 1800, 1828, 1860, 1896, and 1932.

Immediately after the 1980 election, many observers concluded that the decisive Reagan victory (51 percent of the popular vote to 41 percent for Carter), plus the unexpected Republican capture of the Senate and gain of thirty-three seats in the House of Representatives, four governorships, and more than two hundred state legislative seats, meant that 1980 was a realigning election. Moreover social groups that traditionally vote Democratic—including Catholics, blue-collar workers, and voters with no college education—cast their ballots for the Republican nominee, which gave further credence to the contention that the liberal New Deal era in U.S. politics was over and a new Republican majority had finally been formed.[39] When President Reagan embarked successfully on a series of major policy changes, and when by mid-1981 the percentage of voters declaring themselves to be Republicans equaled that of Democrats, some observers became even more convinced that a party realignment had taken place.

Subsequent events, however, indicated that the 1980 election was not a realigning one. As President Reagan began to have problems with the Congress and the economy took a downturn, the number of voters identifying with the Republican party declined, and those declaring themselves to be Democrats rose again until the gap between the two major parties approached its traditional 5-3 ratio. In the 1982 elections the Democrats picked up 26 seats in the House of Representatives, a net gain of 7 governorships, and some 160 additional seats in state legislatures, showing that many Democrats had not permanently deserted their traditional party.

The results of the 1984 presidential election, in which President Reagan captured 59 percent of the popular vote (compared with Mondale's 41 percent) and the electoral votes of forty-nine states (Mondale carried only his home state of Minnesota and the District of Columbia), raised the issue of whether the 1984 election was a realigning one. Several developments were evident in the middle of the 1980s that one would expect to find if a realignment of significant magnitude were occurring: younger voters and newly registered ones tended to be Republicans; many traditional Democrats were deserting the party because they agreed more with the Republicans on issues such as economic growth and opportunity, the necessity of building up the national defense, and social concerns (prayer in the public school, abortion, busing); and the number of political independents appeared to have leveled off or even declined.[10]

Other developments of the mid-1980s, however, did *not* point in the direction of a realigning election. Although President Reagan, himself, won by a large margin in the 1984 election, the Republican party actually lost two seats in the Senate, and the fourteen seats it picked up in the House of Representatives did not compensate for the twenty-six it lost in the 1982 elections. Moreover, despite the presidential landslide, Democrats still controlled thirty-four of the nation's fifty governorships and both houses of the legislature in twenty-eight states, compared with eleven for the Republicans. In late 1985, a Gallup poll found that the Democrats were on the rise again; 40 percent of the American public identified with that party compared with 33 percent who said they were Republicans.[41] Finally, in the 1986 congressional elections, the Democrats unexpectedly picked up 8 seats in the Senate to gain control of that body by a margin of 55 to 45 and added 5 seats in the House of Representatives to increase their numerical superiority over the Republicans to 258-177.

If either the 1980 or 1984 election is compared with the previous realigning elections (1800, 1828, 1860, 1896, and 1932), some major differences appear. The new majority party that emerged in each of these five earlier elections captured not only the presidency but also both houses of Congress (not just the Senate). With the exception of the first instance (1800), the emerging party controlled the House of Representatives in the session preceding the key presidential election (the Republicans did not do that in either 1978 or 1982). Moreover, two years after the presidential race, the new majority party maintained control of both houses of the Congress in what one writer calls "cementing" elections.[42] In contrast, the Republicans in 1982 failed to capture the House of Representatives and in 1986 lost both the Senate and the House to the Democrats. Finally, voting participation generally increased in past realigning elections, but participation in the 1980 election declined from the 1976 contest; and despite the registration efforts of both parties in 1984, voter turnout rose by less than 1 percent that year.

What actually has occurred since the the late 1960s is what Kevin Phillips terms a "split-level" realignment.[43] The Republican party has become the dominant party in presidential elections, capturing four of the last five contests, three of them (1972, 1980, and 1984) by substantial margins. Meanwhile, the Democrats are clearly the majority party in the House of Representatives (the Republicans last controlled that body in the 1953-1955 session). Since 1980 only the Senate can properly be termed a "two-party" institution.

Other analysts, such as Walter Dean Burnham, prefer to characterize the recent era as one of party "decomposition" or "dealignment."[44] Traditional loyalties of the American public to political parties have declined greatly, and therefore the party affiliation of candidates is no longer the principal factor in voting decisions, as it once was. Instead, short-term forces, such as the candidates themselves, issues, events, and incumbent performance, shape how people cast their ballots. As a result, voters switch their votes in presidential elections from one party's candidate to another and split their ballots for different party candidates running for separate offices in the same election. As Burnham explains, "Electoral disaggregation carried beyond a certain point would, after all, make critical realignment in the classical sense impossible."[45]

In mid-1987, the state of U.S. politics appears to be closer to dealignment than to realignment. Recent elections have not constituted a general realignment, as that term has traditionally been used; the Republicans have failed to capture control of both houses of the Congress (along with the presidency), and the prospect of that occurring in the near future seems unlikely. Moreover, while the Republicans were losing eight Senate seats in 1986, they picked up an equal number of governorships from the Democrats, indicating that voters were splitting their ballots, focusing more on evaluations of individual candidates than demonstrating a renewed loyalty to the Democratic party.

The present electoral volatility in U.S. politics significantly influences the president's ability to act as an effective leader of his political party and of the national government in general. Presidential elections also affect another important matter—the making of public policy in the U.S. political system.

Effect on Policy Making

The strongest conceivable influence voters in presidential elections could exercise on policy making in the United States would be to send to the winning candidate a clear message that identified the issues they felt were most important and that defined specific policies the candidate should follow in dealing with those issues. Such a message is called a *mandate*—a set of instructions to the new president on how to govern the nation. As Pomper suggests, the theory of a mandate "has been particularly associated with the Labour party of Great Britain, although it is supported in other nations as well." [46]

For many reasons presidential elections may not meet the requirements of a mandate. As discussed in preceding sections, issues often have little to do with a voter's choice of candidate. Some people vote according to traditional loyalties—they simply choose the candidate who represents the political party with which they identify. Others base their decision on the personal qualities of the competing presidential candidates; they vote for the candidate whose qualities they like or for the opponent of a candidate they dislike (the "lesser of the two evils").

Even when voters choose a candidate because of issues, the election may not produce a mandate. Voters differ on the particular issues they are interested in: some may be concerned over the state of the domestic economy; others, the U.S. position in the world community. Thus, a candidate may garner a plurality of the votes cast by issue-conscious voters, without any single issue having majority support. Moreover, it is one thing for voters to be interested in an issue and quite another for them to be able to suggest specific policies to deal with that issue. Finally, individual policies favored by voters may conflict with one another. Voters may favor, for example, increased government expenditures for national defense but also support a tax cut and a balanced budget. If it proves to be impossible to carry out all these policies simultaneously (as was true during Reagan's presidency), the electorate may provide no clear message on which policy has the highest priority.

The failure of a presidential election to produce a mandate does not mean that it has no implications for public policy making in the United

States. As one observer explains, elections are in effect a "retrospective" judgment on the performance of the incumbent officeholder.[47] When voters reelect the officeholder, they are showing their general satisfaction with the way his administration has been handling the principal issues facing the country. Voters may also use this evaluation of past performance to shape their expectations of a president's future performance.[48] In 1984, for example, people who voted for President Reagan approved of the way he had handled major problems (especially the economy) and assumed he would continue to handle those problems successfully in the next four years. Yet they gave little guidance on the specific policies the administration should follow. As discussed in a preceding section, on several major issues the electorate more often agreed with Mondale than with Reagan. Moreover, in the 1984 campaign the president made few specific promises about how he would address the major issue of the economy (the budget deficit), except to say that he would raise taxes only as a "last resort." Thus, a vote to keep a president in office is primarily a favorable judgment both on his past performance and on the prospects of achieving particular *outcomes* (such as a prosperous economy); it is not an assessment of the *means,* that is, the specific policies, necessary to reach those outcomes.

In retrospective voting, the voters oust an administration from office primarily because they are so dissatisfied with its past performance and so pessimistic about its future performance that they are willing to give the winning opponent the opportunity to do a better job. Beyond this message, however, a presidential election offers a new president little guidance. The electorate indicates the general *goal* that it wants the president to achieve rather than the policies he should follow to reach that goal. In the 1968 election the voters did not instruct Richard Nixon to follow any particular course of action in extricating the nation from Vietnam, but they did give him the message that he should somehow reach that goal. The electoral message also may suggest that the new president should not continue to follow the policies of his predecessor on the issue. It may also indicate the *general direction* of the public policies the newly elected president should pursue. For example, Warren Miller feels that the 1980 presidential election not only constituted a negative assessment of the performance of President Carter in office but also expressed a general preference for more conservative policies on government spending and on the scope of government services and support for a major reduction in federal income taxes, among other matters. Miller makes it clear, however, that the election did not provide a mandate for President Reagan's specific positions on each issue.[49]

Aside from the question of what policy directions (if any) presidential elections offer successful candidates, presidents themselves frequently interpret the election results as a mandate to pursue policies that they personally favor. As presidential advisor George Reedy put it, "President Johnson and most of his close advisors interpreted the election result [the 1964 landslide victory of Johnson over Goldwater] as a mandate from the people not only to carry on the policies of the Johnson administration but any other policies that might come to mind." [50] The same tendency applies when the candidate of the party out of power wins an election. When Ronald Reagan assumed the presidency after his victory over Jimmy Carter in 1980, he claimed a mandate from the people to embark on a broad range of conservative policies, some of which—such as reduced rates of government expenditures on health, educatior, and environmental protection and opposition to the Equal Rights Amendment and abortion—ran counter to voters' preferences.

The indefinite guidance the electorate offers the winner of presidential elections gives the president great freedom in initiating public policies. In recent years new presidents often have sought to have enacted the pledges made in their party platforms.[51] Moreover, both Lyndon Johnson and Richard Nixon acted on more than half of the promises they made in campaign speeches in 1964 and 1968,[52] as did Dwight Eisenhower and John Kennedy on the promises they made in their 1952 and 1960 campaigns.[53] A positive relationship does exist, therefore, between what presidential candidates say they will do if elected and the policies they actually follow after they assume office, whether or not the electorate supports them for that reason.

At the same time, U.S. presidents must strive to keep their policies in line with the preferences of the voters. If their new policies go further than their electoral supporters intended, or even if the admittedly favored policies do not turn out to be successful, presidents face the possibility of being ousted from office at the next election. As political scientist V. O. Key points out, "Governments must worry, not about the meaning of past elections, but about their fate at future elections." This means that "the electorate can exert a prospective influence if not control" over government policy.[54]

The type of presidential election has some bearing on the policies enacted after the election. Maintaining elections not only keep the majority party in power but typically result in the continuation of its policies, which have met the general approval of the electorate. Deviating elections provide the opportunity for some change in policies but not a radical departure from the past. The Eisenhower administration, for example, slowed down and modified some of the policies of previous Democratic administrations, but it did not try to repeal the New Deal.

115

Realigning elections (or eras) typically result in major changes in public policy. An analysis of the statutes enacted from 1789 to 1968 shows that those passed in the period immediately following a realigning election departed most from policies of the past.[55]

Notes

1. 238 U.S. 347 (1915).
2. 321 U.S. 649 (1944).
3. 295 U.S. 45 (1935).
4. In *Harper v. Virginia State Board of Elections* 383 U.S. 663 (1966), the Supreme Court eliminated the payment of a poll tax as a requirement for voting in state elections by ruling that it violated the equal protection clause of the Fourteenth Amendment.
5. A major issue was whether voting rights violations should require actual proof of the "intent" to discriminate (as favored by the Reagan administration), or whether it was sufficient that an election law or procedure merely "result" in discrimination (as favored by civil rights groups). Sen. Robert Dole (R-Kans.) took the leadership in developing an acceptable compromise on the issue.
6. Although Reagan defeated Carter by almost 10 percentage points (51-41), it was not until the last weekend before the election that the polls showed Reagan to be outdistancing the incumbent president.
7. Paul R. Abramson, John H. Aldrich, and David W. Rhode, *Change and Continuity in the 1980 Elections* (Washington, D.C.: CQ Press, 1982), chap. 4.
8. Angus Campbell, Philip Converse, Warren Miller, and Donald Stokes, *The American Voter,* abr. ed. (New York: Wiley, 1964).
9. Philip Converse, *The Dynamics of Party Support: Cohort-Analyzing Party Identification* (Beverly Hills: Sage, 1976), 34.
10. V. O. Key, *The Responsible Electorate: Rationality in Presidential Voting* (Cambridge, Mass.: Belknap Press, 1966).
11. Based on data provided by the University of Michigan Center for Political Studies.
12. One possible reason for the high percentage of ticket splitting between presidential and House races in 1980 was the presence of independent John Anderson in the presidential contest that year. In most states Anderson's supporters did not have the option of voting for an independent House candidate.
13. Norman Nie, Sidney Verba, and John Petrocik, *The Changing American Voter* (Cambridge, Mass.: Harvard University Press, 1979), chap. 4.
14. Campbell et al., *The American Voter,* 83-85.
15. Gerald Pomper, *Voter's Choice: Varieties of American Electoral Behavior* (New York: Dodd, Mead, 1975), chap. 2.
16. Nie, Verba, and Petrocik, *Changing American Voter,* 70-72.
17. Converse, *Dynamics of Party Support,* chap. 4.
18. For the 1940 election, Paul Lazarsfeld, Bernard Berelson, and Hazel Gaudt, *The People's Choice* (New York: Columbia University Press, 1944); for the

1948 election, Paul Lazarsfeld, Bernard Berelson, and William McPhee, *Voting* (Chicago: University of Chicago Press, 1954).

19. It should be pointed out that one reason for the Reagan increases was the absence in 1984 of a third party candidate, such as John Anderson, to drain off votes. This factor also contributed to Mondale's winning a greater percentage of votes than Carter did among several groups, although only that of white-collar workers exceeded 5 percent.

20. Warren Miller and Teresa Levitin, *Leadership and Change: The New Politics and the American Electorate* (Cambridge, Mass.: Winthrop, 1976), 42.

21. Herbert Asher, *Presidential Elections and American Politics: Voters, Candidates and Campaigns since 1952* (Homewood, Ill.: Dorsey, 1976), chap. 5.

22. J. Merrill Shanks and Warren Miller, "Policy Direction and Performance Evaluation: Complementary Explanations of the Reagan Elections" (Paper delivered at the annual meeting of the American Political Science Association, New Orleans, August 29-September 1, 1985), 60, 69.

23. Campbell et al., *The American Voter*, chap. 7.

24. Pomper, *Voter's Choice.*

25. Nie, Verba, and Petrocik, *The Changing American Voter.*

26. Pomper, *Voter's Choice*, chap. 8.

27. Nie, Verba, and Petrocik, *The Changing American Voter*, chap. 7.

28. Philip Converse, "The Nature of Belief Systems in Mass Publics," in *Ideology and Discontent,* ed. David Apter (New York: Free Press, 1964).

29. Norman Nie and Kristi Anderson, "Mass Belief Systems Revisited: Political Change and Attitude Structure," *The Journal of Politics* (August 1974): 540-591.

30. Arthur Miller and Warren Miller, "Partisanship and Performance: Rational Choice in the 1976 Presidential Election" (Paper delivered at the annual meeting of the American Political Science Association, Washington, D.C., September 1-4, 1977).

31. Arthur Miller, "Policy and Performance Voting in the 1980 Election" (Paper delivered at the annual meeting of the American Political Science Association, New York, September 3-6, 1981).

32. Warren Miller, "Policy Directions and Presidential Leadership: Alternative Interpretations of the 1980 Presidential Election" (Paper delivered at the annual meeting of the American Political Science Association, New York, September 3-6, 1981).

33. Abramson, Aldrich, and Rohde, *Change and Continuity in the 1980 Elections.*

34. Martin Wattenberg, "The Hollow Realignment: Partisan Change in a Candidate-Centered Era" (Paper delivered at the annual meeting of the American Political Science Association, New Orleans, August 29-September 1, 1985).

35. Paul R. Abramson, John H. Aldrich, and David W. Rohde, *Change and Continuity in the 1984 Elections,* rev. ed. (Washington, D.C.: CQ Press, 1987), chap. 6.

36. Shanks and Miller, "Policy Direction and Performance Evaluation."

37. Campbell et al., *The American Voter*, chap. 16.

38. Analysts refer to an election following a deviating period as a *reinstating* one, because it reinstates the usual majority party. Examples are the 1960 and 1976 elections, when the Democrats returned to power after the two Eisen-

hower and the two Nixon victories. A reinstating election, therefore, is like a maintaining one in that long-term partisan factors determine the result.

39. See Kevin Phillips, *The Emerging Republican Majority* (New Rochelle, N.Y.: Arlington House, 1969).
40. Thomas Cavanaugh and James Sundquist, "The New Two-Party System" in *The New Direction in American Politics,* ed. John Chubb and Paul Peterson (Washington, D.C.: Brookings, 1985), chap. 2.
41. *The Gallup Report,* October-November 1985, 42-44.
42. Wattenberg, "The Hollow Realignment," 4.
43. This term is used in Phillips's biweekly newsletter, *The American Political Report* (January 11, 1985), as cited in Abramson, Aldrich, and Rohde, *Change and Continuity in the 1984 Elections,* 287.
44. Walter Dean Burnham, *Critical Elections and the Mainsprings of American Politics* (New York: Norton, 1970), chap. 5.
45. Ibid., 91-92.
46. Gerald Pomper, with Susan Lederman, *Elections in America: Control and Influence in Democratic Politics,* 2d ed. (New York: Longman, 1980), 212.
47. V. O. Key, Jr., *The Responsible Electorate: Rationality in Presidential Voting* (Cambridge, Mass.: Belknap Press, 1966).
48. Anthony Downs, *An Economic Theory of Democracy* (New York: Harper and Row, 1957); and Morris Fiorina, *Retrospective Voting in American National Elections* (New Haven: Yale University Press, 1981).
49. Miller, "Policy Directions and Presidential Leadership."
50. George Reedy, *The Twilight of the Presidency* (New York: New American Library, 1970), 66.
51. Pomper, *Elections in America,* chap. 8.
52. Fred Grogan, "Candidate Promise and Presidential Performance" (Paper delivered at the annual meeting of the Midwest Political Science Association, Chicago, April 21-23, 1977).
53. Arnold John Muller, "Public Policy and the Presidential Election Process: A Study of Promise and Performance" (Ph.D. diss., University of Missouri-Columbia, 1986).
54. Key, *The Responsible Electorate,* 77.
55. Benjamin Ginsberg, "Elections and Public Policy," *American Political Science Review* (March 1976): 41-49.

Selected Readings

Campbell, Angus, Philip Converse, Warren Miller, and Donald Stokes. *The American Voter.* abr. ed. New York: Wiley, 1964.
Key, V. O., Jr. *The Responsible Electorate: Rationality in Presidential Voting.* Cambridge, Mass.: Belknap Press, 1966.
Miller, Warren, and Teresa Levitin. *Leadership and Change: The New Politics and the American Electorate.* Cambridge, Mass.: Winthrop, 1976.
Nie, Norman, Sidney Verba, and John Petrocik. *The Changing American Voter.* Cambridge Mass.: Harvard University Press, 1979.
Pomper, Gerald, with Susan Lederman. *Elections in America: Control and Influence in Democratic Politics.* 2d ed. New York: Longman, 1980.

Summary and Assessment of Presidential Contests 5

This final chapter summarizes and assesses major changes that have occurred in the selection of the president in recent years and suggests ways in which the selection process should be reformed to make it more democratic and more effective. The first section focuses on the nomination of the president; the second, on the election of the chief executive.

The Nomination of the President

Over the years, significant changes have occurred in the procedure for selecting the persons who represent the major parties in the general election contest. Initially, party leaders in the Congress used congressional caucuses to designate their nominees. Then, for a brief period, the parties turned to state legislatures and conventions to propose favorite-son candidates before moving to a new institution, the national convention, to choose their presidential candidates. Although this method prevails today, the advent of presidential primaries has altered it greatly. Thus, the presidential nomination process has been progressively democratized as the participants have changed from party elites to the general public itself. Through primaries, the public indirectly affects the process by helping determine the composition of the national convention that officially names the presidential candidate.

The changes that occurred from the early days of the nation's history until the mid-1960s, nearly two centuries, were gradual; those that have occurred since then have been abrupt. From 1968 to 1980, what political scientist Byron Shafer calls a "quiet revolution" took place in the process by which the parties (especially the Democrats) chose their presidential candidates.[1] Alterations in the rules of the game transferred the choice of candidates from caucus-conventions dominated by public and party officials to popular primaries in which an increasing number of rank-and-file voters choose delegates for the national convention who are pledged to support specific presidential candidates. In addition, the private financing of nomination campaigns by large contributors gave way to a system of government subsidies that match the donations of small donors. New political elites also emerged: political amateurs and members of the media replaced professionals, such as governors, senators, House members, and state party leaders, as the most influential people in the nomination of presidential candidates. Moreover, as Shafer points out, the new political elites spoke for a white-collar electorate in contrast to the blue-collar rank-and-file voters, represented mainly by the professionals.[2]

The 1980s have witnessed a "counterrevolution" in nomination politics. Between 1980 and 1984, six states abandoned presidential primaries in favor of caucus-conventions.[3] Consequently, the proportion of national convention delegates chosen in primaries fell from almost three-fourths to slightly more than half. Professionals were brought back into the nomination process in the form of superdelegates, constituting one of seven delegates at the 1984 Democratic national convention. In the battle over the 1988 rules, the professionals once more prevailed over the amateurs, as the number of superdelegates was increased.

The result of this revolution and counterrevolution—created by two decades of continual reform in the Democratic party—is a mixed nomination system. It incorporates the selection of delegates by both the primary and caucus-convention methods. The participants include professionals representing blue-collar constituents, such as organized labor, as well as amateurs, who speak largely for white-collar constituents. Indeed, the 1984 nomination process reflected these differences: Mondale generally was favored by party professionals, Democratic loyalists, blue-collar workers, and older people; and Hart, by amateurs, political independents, white-collar workers, and younger voters. The presidential nomination system reflects alterations in the rules of the game as well as the significant political changes that resulted from those alterations.

This mixed nomination system is, in my opinion, a desirable one. It provides a judicious blend of political amateurs, primarily concerned with the candidates' stands on issues, and party professionals, who bring distinctive "peer" perspectives to bear on the candidates' ability to work effectively with other public officials with whom they must share the governance of the nation. Professionals also consider how successful candidates are likely to be in helping to compromise the differences that exist among the many increasingly assertive groups in U.S. society. At the same time, the presidential primaries place a premium on candidates who possess the personality and communications skills needed to attract the support of rank-and-file voters.

The sequence of state contests in 1988 probably again will give Iowa and New Hampshire too much influence simply because they are likely to hold their caucus-convention and primary sooner than any of the other states. It now appears, however, that a "Super Tuesday" in early March 1988 will include even more southern states than in 1984 and that several midwestern states will hold their state contests on a common date soon after that. It remains to be seen just what the final schedule will be and what effect the Iowa and New Hampshire contests will have on the fortunes of the candidates in later contests. These developments offer the distinct possibility, however, that presidential hopefuls will be required to establish early on their political appeal in a broad range of states rather than in only small and somewhat unrepresentative ones, such as Iowa and New Hampshire. Thus, a pattern of regional contests, long advocated by many critics of the presidential nomination process, has resulted from decisions made at the state level without the necessity of a national law on the matter.

Finally, problems still exist in the way the mass media cover the nomination process. The media continue to concentrate on the "horse race" aspect of the campaign and devote little effort to giving in-depth information on the issues of the campaign or the records of candidates in their previous offices. One mitigating factor is the recent development of debates among the competing candidates, the Republicans in 1980 and the Democrats in 1984. Such encounters enable the voters to judge the candidates' ability to think on their feet and to see how the participants handle common questions (in regular campaign speeches, the candidates frequently talk past one another).

Thus, although the nomination process is far from ideal, it has undergone some change for the better, particularly in the 1980s. Moreover, there is little one can do about some of the problems, such as the way the media in a free society choose to cover the campaign. Finally, as the recent record of the Democratic party demonstrates, there is real danger in constantly revising the rules of the game: unintended and unfortunate consequences often result from such changes.[4] Everyone involved would benefit from a needed hiatus in the quest for perfection in the presidential nomination process.

The Election of the President

Recent changes in the election of the president have not been as sweeping as the changes in the nomination process; however, two in particular have had a significant effect on the general election process. The first has to do with the financing of presidential contests, and the second pertains to the increased use of candidate debates in the fall campaign.

The public financing of presidential elections has the advantages of equalizing the resources available to the two major party candidates and of sparing them the potential abuses associated with raising funds from large contributors. However, new, minor candidates (such as John Anderson in 1980) must wait until after the election to determine whether they will receive any public subsidy (a person must win at least 5 percent of the popular vote to so qualify), a requirement that makes it difficult for them to raise money when it is most needed—during the campaign itself. The law should be changed to provide public funds for candidates who reach a certain level of support in the public opinion polls (such as 15 percent) at some designated time during the campaign.

Recent debates have also benefited presidential elections by helping to acquaint the electorate with the candidates' views on a variety of political issues. They also enable the vast audience to judge the personal qualities of the participants. I would, however, suggest two ways of improving such debates. First, their format should be changed so that other knowledgeable persons besides journalists, such as economists, political scientists, or public officials, are included among the questioners; moreover, the candidates themselves should be allowed to ask questions of one another. Second, persons should *not* have the option of refusing to participate in a debate on the grounds that it might hurt their candidacy (as Carter did in the first 1980 debate, which included Reagan and Anderson). Since the major purpose of presidential debates is the education of the electorate, not the strengthening or weakening of a particular candidacy, agreement to participate in debates should be made a condition for the receipt of federal campaign funds. (Admittedly, presidential debates to date appear to have been to the advantage of the challenger, but even if that is so, it would seem to compensate for the many other electoral advantages enjoyed by the incumbent.)

The most serious problem pertaining to the election of the president continues to be the electoral college. It was devised as a means of allowing knowledgeable elites in the states to choose a "continental" character, but its essential form remains for an entirely different purpose—to enable rank-and-file voters to select their major public officials in a nationwide popular election. As a result of this perversion, several abuses have developed in the presidential election system.

The electoral college as it operates today violates some of the major tenets of political equality. Each person's vote does not count equally: the influence one has in the election of the president depends on the political situation in one's particular state. For the many Americans who support a losing candidate in their state, it is as though they had not voted at all, since under the general-ticket system all the electoral votes of a state go to the candidate who wins a plurality of its popular votes. Other citizens who live in populous, politically competitive states have a premium placed on their vote because they are in a position to affect how large blocs of electoral votes are cast. Nor does the electoral college ensure that the candidate who receives the most popular votes will win the presidency: John Quincy Adams in 1824, Rutherford B. Hayes in 1876, and Benjamin Harrison in 1888 went to the White House even though they trailed their respective political opponents, Andrew Jackson, Samuel Tilden, and Grover Cleveland. In 1976 Jimmy Carter almost suffered the same fate as Jackson, Tilden, and Cleveland: if some nine thousand voters in Hawaii and Ohio had shifted their ballots to President Ford, Ford would have edged out Carter in the electoral college, 270-268.

The requirement that a candidate win a majority of the electoral votes or have the election decided by the House of Representatives also violates the idea of political equality. In 1948 Harry S Truman defeated Thomas Dewey by more than two million popular votes, but if some twelve thousand people in California and Ohio had voted for Dewey rather than the president, the election would have been thrown into the House of Representatives for a decision. The same thing could have happened in 1960 if some nine thousand people in Illinois and Missouri had voted for Richard Nixon instead of John F. Kennedy, and again in 1968 if about forty-two thousand people in Missouri, New Jersey, and Alaska had cast their ballots for Hubert Humphrey rather than President Nixon.[5] Permitting the House of Representatives, voting by states, to select the president of the United States is not consistent with the "one person, one vote" principle.

The 1968 election also illustrates another danger of the electoral college system: an elector need not cast his or her ballot for the candidate who wins the plurality of votes in the elector's state. Had Nixon failed to win a majority of the electoral votes, third-party candidate George Wallace would have been in a position to bargain with him. Wallace could have asked his forty-five electors to cast their ballots for Nixon, which would have given Nixon enough electoral votes to prevent the election from going into the House.[6] Although Wallace's forty-five electoral votes would not have been enough to give Humphrey a majority of the electoral votes (even if Humphrey had carried Missouri, New Jersey, and Alaska), the Alabama governor could have tried to bargain with him by offering to influence southern members of the House of Representatives to chose Humphrey over Nixon.

Over the years these problems have created a great deal of dissatisfaction with the electoral college. The sentiment for changing it has increased recently, particularly after the elections of 1948, 1960, 1968, and 1976, in which a switch in votes of a relatively few people in key states would have sent the selection of the president into the House or immediately changed the result. Although agreement on the need to change the electoral college is widespread, there is marked disagreement over what form that change should take. Five plans have been suggested as substitutes for the present system.

The first, known as the *automatic plan,* which would change the present system least, would eliminate the possibility of "faithless electors" by abolishing that office and automatically casting a state's electoral votes for the popular-vote winner in that state. If no candidate received a majority of the electoral votes, a joint session of Congress would choose the winner, and each representative and senator would have one vote.

The second, known as the *district plan,* proposes a return to the method the states used early in the nation's history (and that was recently reinstated by Maine), under which the presidential candidate who wins the plurality vote in each House district would receive its electoral vote, with the remaining two electoral votes going to the statewide popular winner. If no candidate received a majority of the electoral votes, senators and representatives, sitting jointly and voting as individuals, would choose the president from the three candidates having the highest number of electoral votes. This plan's major supporters have been members of Congress and private groups from rural areas, such as the American Farm Bureau. If the plan were adopted, the crucial areas would be the politically competitive congressional districts where the two major parties traditionally divide the vote 55 to 45 percent.

A third proposal, known as the *proportional plan,* would divide each state's electoral votes in proportion to the division of the popular vote: a candidate receiving 60 percent of the popular vote in a state would receive 60 percent of its electoral votes. A plan of this nature, introduced by Republican senator Henry Cabot Lodge of Massachusetts and Democratic representative Ed Gossett of Texas, passed the Senate in 1950 but failed to be enacted by the House. The plan would eliminate the present advantage of the large states in being able to throw all their electoral votes to one candidate and has therefore been opposed by many of their legislators, including John Kennedy when he was a senator from Massachusetts. One possible consequence of a proportional division of the electoral votes would be a fairly even split between the two major candidates so that neither would receive a majority; hence, there would be a greater likelihood of elections being thrown into the House for decision.[7]

The fourth plan, *direct popular election* of the president, has picked up major support in recent years, especially since its recommendation in 1967 by a special commission of the American Bar Association. In addition, it has been endorsed by politically disparate groups such as the Chamber of Commerce of the United States and the AFL-CIO (American Federation of Labor and Congress of Industrial Organizations). In 1969 the House passed a constitutional amendment providing that the president (and vice president) be elected by a minimum of 40 percent of the popular vote and, if no candidate received so large a vote, that a runoff be held between the two leading contenders. The Senate failed to pass the amendment, however, despite the efforts of its major sponsor, Birch Bayh (D-Ind.). After Carter's narrow electoral college victory, Bayh introduced the same measure in 1977, but it failed to clear the Congress that year. No such proposal subsequently has been enacted.

A fifth proposal, recently advanced by the Twentieth Century Fund, a research group, is known as the *national bonus plan*.[8] It would award the nationwide popular winner 102 "bonus" votes (2 for each state plus 2 for the District of Columbia), which would be added to the electoral votes received under the present state-by-state system. To win the election a candidate would have to receive 321 votes, that is, a majority of 640, the new total number of the electoral votes (538, the former total, plus the 102 bonus votes). If no one received a majority of the electoral votes, a runoff would be held between the two front-runners. Thus, the proposal retains the electoral college system but makes the total electoral vote better reflect the nationwide popular vote. It also allows the voters rather than the House of Representatives to make the final choice of the president if no candidate receives a majority of the electoral votes.

In my judgment, the first three plans have serious defects. The automatic plan meets only the problem of the faithless elector and ignores several others: the undue influence of the very small and very large states; the winner-take-all principle by which all the electoral votes of a state go to the candidate who wins a plurality of the popular votes, no matter how narrow that margin may be; and the possibility of a person's winning the presidency even though he trails his opponent in the nationwide popular vote. The district plan would incorporate into the selection of the president the gerrymandering abuses present in elections to the House of Representatives—manipulation of district boundaries to favor particular political interests. The proportional plan would eliminate the winner-take-all advantage now enjoyed by the large states but would retain the small-state benefit, because all states, regardless of size, would receive two electoral votes representing their two senators. It also would not prevent the possibility of a minority-vote president.

The last two plans, the direct popular election of the president and the national bonus plan, provide the most promising prospects for reform. Direct popular election ensures what none of the other plans can: that the person receiving the largest number of nationwide popular votes will be elected president. The national bonus plan makes it much more likely than does the present system that the popular-vote winner also will obtain a majority of the electoral votes but *does not guarantee it*. By retaining elements of the present state-by-state electoral system, how-ever, the bonus plan incorporates features of federalism that are not present under the direct popular election plan.

Either direct popular election or the national bonus plan would be, in my judgment, far superior to the present system. Of the two, I prefer direct popular election because it guarantees that the national popular-vote winner will be chosen as president. Although the national bonus system does retain the state-by-state feature of the present system, sufficient elements of federalism already are contained in the U.S. political system through the equal representation of the states in the Senate and in the arrangement of separate state powers and political institutions whose independence is guaranteed from national encroach-ment by the Constitution. I see no reason why federalism should also require that states be represented as electoral units in the selection of the major national official.

Arguments can be made against the direct popular election of the president. Some analysts contend that it will jeopardize the two-party system, a fear based on two separate considerations. The first is that, since the election will depend on a nationwide instead of a state-by-state vote, candidates will no longer need to deal with state political leaders. This change would weaken these leaders, who have traditionally played a vital role in American political parties. The second concern, expressed by Alexander Bickel, is that direct popular election of the president would encourage minor political parties, freed of the necessity of actually winning state electoral votes, to run and support enough candidates to prevent either major party nominee from the necessary 40 percent of the nationwide popular vote.[9] These minor parties would then be in a bargaining position to determine which of the two leading candidates would win in the runoff election.

I believe these fears are unfounded. State party leaders would continue to play a role in presidential nominations. It is even possible that they would become more active in the general election under a popular election system, since all votes that they could muster would count in their candidate's nationwide total. I also think it highly improbable that the winning party candidate would not be able to win 40 percent of the popular vote. As Lawrence Longley and Alan Braun point out,[10] in the presidential elections held since 1824, only Abraham Lincoln in 1860 failed to achieve that proportion (he won 39.8 percent of the vote).[11] If anything, the electoral college system is more vulnerable to minor parties than is the popular election system, because in the United States such parties tend to be regional and thus are best able to affect the distribution of electoral votes of individual states. A case in point occurred in New York in 1976. Many observers maintain that if independent candidate Eugene J. McCarthy had been on the ballot in New York, he would have drained away enough popular votes from Carter to allow Ford to carry the state and, with it, enough electoral votes (forty-one) to win the presidential election.

Another significant problem of the direct election system is the effect that its adoption might have on the nomination process.[12] As Austin Ranney suggests, most of the arguments made against the electoral college and in favor of direct national election can also be made against national party conventions and in favor of a direct national primary.[13] Both the electoral college and the national conventions violate the one-person, one-vote rule, make it possible to choose a candidate preferred by a minority, and place artificial barriers between the people and their choice of candidates. Although Ranney does not make the point explicitly, it might well be argued that the adoption of the direct election of the president would lead in time to enactment of a national primary law; for historically, the number of a state's electoral votes has affected the size of its delegation to national conventions. In this way, the selection and nomination processes have been linked, and tampering with one might influence the other.

The last possibility gives me the greatest cause for concern since I do not favor the adoption of a national primary that could further diminish the influence of political leaders in the nomination process. I do think, however, that the two processes are distinct, and changing one does not necessarily mean altering the other. Moving from the electoral college system to a direct popular election of the president would not be nearly so radical a change as abandoning the convention system for a national presidential primary. Direct popular election would not significantly change the method of selection or the people participating in the election of the president; it merely would change *how the votes are counted.* A change in the presidential nominating system, however, would impose a whole new method of selection and bring into the process people who are not now eligible to vote in presidential primaries. Such a change also

127

would require a new means of choosing vice-presidential candidates and of adopting the party platform. It would, it is hoped, be much more difficult to persuade political decision makers to adopt a national primary than to adopt direct popular election of the president. A diverse range of groups favors direct election of the president, but the idea of a national primary has no broad support. Moreover, the House has approved direct election, but Congress has not given serious consideration to a national primary.

The known defects of the present electoral college system must be weighed against the possible dangers that the direct election of the president might bring, particularly its potential effect on the nomination process. Still, I would be willing to take the gamble of a change. I cannot see the wisdom of perpetuating an electoral system that in 1976 almost permitted an appointed chief executive, who lost his only presidential election by almost 2 million votes, to remain in office another term. The U.S. political system, already subject to a great deal of cynicism by the American people, should not have to bear that additional threat to its legitimacy.

Notes

1. Byron E. Shafer, *Quiet Revolution: The Struggle for the Democratic Party and the Shaping of the Post-Reform Politics* (New York: Russell Sage Foundation, 1983).
2. Ibid., 524.
3. Although the information on the 1988 contest is incomplete at this time (August 1987), it appears that there will be a movement back toward more state primaries in 1988.
4. A book dealing with such consequences is Nelson Polsby, *Consequences of Party Reform* (New York: Oxford University Press, 1983).
5. In each of these elections, persons other than the two major party candidates received electoral votes. The losing candidates, Dewey, Nixon, and Humphrey, therefore could have carried the key states named in the text and still not have had a majority of the electoral votes.
6. Although Wallace actually earned forty-five electoral votes, he received forty-six because one elector in North Carolina (which went for Nixon) cast his vote for the Alabama governor. In 1960, 1972, and 1976, single electors in Oklahoma, Virginia, and Washington also did not cast their ballots for the candidate receiving the popular-vote plurality in their state.
7. Most of the proportional plans have suggested lowering the winning electoral-vote requirement from a majority to 40 or even 35 percent to avoid the possibility of having the election go to the House. They have also proposed that, if no candidate receives the requisite proportion of electoral votes, the two houses, meeting jointly and voting as individuals, choose the president.

8. *Winner-Take-All: Report of the Twentieth Century Task Force on Reform of the Presidential Election Process* (New York: Holmes and Meier, 1978), 4-6.

9. Alexander Bickel, *The New Age of Political Reform: The Electoral College, the Convention, and the Party System* (New York: Harper and Row, 1968), 14-16.

10. Lawrence Longley and Alan Braun, *The Politics of Electoral College Reform* (New Haven: Yale University Press, 1975), chap. 2.

11. Neal Peirce, *The People's President: The Electoral College in American History and the Direct-Vote Alternative* (New York: Simon and Schuster, 1968), 295, also cites figures compiled by Donald Stokes showing that in 170 gubernatorial elections occurring in the thirty most competitive states between 1952 and 1964 (these contests, of course, were based on a direct popular vote), the winning candidate never received less than 40 percent of the popular vote.

12. I do not find significant the argument that the electoral college is desirable because it presently amplifies close popular election outcomes (Martin Diamond, *The Electoral College and the American Idea of Democracy* [Washington, D.C.: American Enterprise Institute, 1977], 16). The same is true of the contention that direct popular election would increase the possibility of vote fraud (Judith Best, *The Case against the Direct Election of the President: A Defense of the Electoral College* [Ithaca, N.Y.: Cornell University Press, 1975], chap. 6). Justifying a distortion of the actual election results to create a false mandate seems curious. Moreover, the effects of vote fraud are more likely to be felt at the state than the national level; in 1976, nine thousand false ballots in Hawaii and Ohio could have reversed Carter's electoral victory, but it would have taken almost one hundred times that number to have eliminated his 1.7 million nationwide popular plurality.

13. Austin Ranney, *The Federalization of Presidential Primaries* (Washington, D.C.: American Enterprise Institute, 1978), 4.

Appendixes:
Guide to the 1988
Presidential Race ⎯⎯⎯⎯⎯⎯

Schedule of
1988 Presidential
Primaries and Caucuses A

The primary and caucus dates below constitute the schedule as of August 31, 1987. States that select Republican and Democratic delegates on different dates are designated by a "D" or an "R." States listed in normal type are holding caucuses; states listed in **bold** type are holding primaries.

Feb. 8	Iowa		**Virginia**
Feb. 16	**New Hampshire**		Washington
Feb. 23	Minnesota	March 10	American Samoa (D)
	South Dakota		Alaska (D)
Feb. 28	Maine (D)	March 12	South Carolina (D)
March 1	**Vermont (non-**	March 13	North Dakota (D)
	binding)	March 15	**Illinois**
March 5	**South Carolina (R)**	March 19	Kansas (D)
	Wyoming	March 20	**Puerto Rico**
March 8	**Alabama**	March 22	**Democrats Abroad** [b]
	Arkansas	March 26	Michigan (D)
	Florida	March 29	**Connecticut**
	Georgia	April 2	Virgin Islands (D)
	Hawaii (D)	April 4	Colorado
	Idaho (D)	April 5	**Wisconsin**
	Kentucky	April 16	Arizona (D)
	Louisiana	April 18	Delaware (D)
	Maryland	April 19	**New York**
	Massachusetts		Vermont (D)
	Mississippi	April 24	Guam
	Missouri	April 25	Utah
	Nevada (D)	April 26	Vermont (R)
	North Carolina		**Pennsylvania**
	Oklahoma	May 3	**District of Columbia**
	Rhode Island		**Indiana**
	Tennessee		**Ohio**
	Texas [a]	May 10	**Nebraska**

The Presidential Contest

	West Virginia		Montana
May 17	Oregon		New Jersey
May 24	Idaho		New Mexico
June 7	California	June 14	North Dakota

Source: *Congressional Quarterly Weekly Report,* August 29, 1987.

a Democratic and Republican primaries and a Democratic caucus are held in Texas on Super Tuesday. The Democratic primary is non-binding. Democratic delegates are selected at the caucus that evening.
b Any U.S. citizen of voting age who lives abroad may participate in the March 22 mail-in primary collectively designated "Democrats Abroad."

Profiles of Major Candidates in the 1988 Presidential Contest ═══ B

Democrats

1. Bruce Babbitt, lawyer

Formerly the state attorney general and governor of Arizona, Babbitt worked successfully with a legislature dominated by Republicans in a Sunbelt state controlled by the GOP. He is most proud of the groundwater management and Medicaid programs he developed there. Once a civil rights and social activist, he now believes that government tries to do too much and insists that it must set limits on its activities and establish priorities among them. He also advocates that all government programs be based on "need" and not offered broadly to members of the middle class. As governor, he antagonized labor by calling out the National Guard in 1983 to protect nonunion workers during a strike in the copper industry. He opposes military aid to the contras but approves of the actions of the Reagan administration in Grenada and Libya. He is often compared with Jimmy Carter because of his non-Washington perspective, his penchant for details, and his conviction about the rightness of his actions.

2. Joseph Biden, lawyer, U.S. senator from Delaware

Biden is a self-proclaimed representative of the "baby boom" generation of voters under forty years of age. He feels that its members became disillusioned with government because of "wrong" decisions about Vietnam, Watergate, and the energy crisis but that its dreams can be recaptured by "right" ones, such as the signing of an arms control agreement with the Soviets. He is highly critical of the Democratic party's catering to special interests and argues that it must concern itself

Information available as of August 1987; subject to change.

with the problems of the middle class as well as those of the poor. Although Biden's voting record is generally liberal, he does not support busing to achieve integration or the federal funding of abortion, and he favors the Gramm-Rudman-Hollings plan to reduce the budget and a tough program against crime. As chairperson of the Senate Judiciary Committee, he has opposed some of President Reagan's nominations to the federal courts. An emotional and effective speaker, he sometimes is accused of lacking "substance" in his approach to public problems.

3. Michael Dukakis, lawyer, governor of Massachusetts

Dukakis, the son of a poor Greek immigrant who went on to become a highly successful doctor, is serving his third term as governor of Massachusetts. Dukakis takes credit for turning around the state economy from one of high taxes, high unemployment, and low growth. First elected governor in 1974, Dukakis oversaw the largest tax increase in the state's history, which led to his defeat in the 1978 Democratic primary by a conservative, Edward King, who campaigned on an antitax platform. In 1982, however, Dukakis came back to defeat King (whose administration was marred by scandal). The income-tax increase imposed in Dukakis's first term had been abolished, and in his second term a program that improved collection of existing taxes brought fiscal health to the state, which now has low unemployment as well. Dukakis also embarked on a successful program of industrial growth based on a cooperative arrangement among government, business, labor, and the academic community. Reelected in 1986 by a wide margin, Dukakis is expected to win the first primary in the neighboring state of New Hampshire.

4. Richard A. Gephardt, lawyer, U.S. representative from Missouri

The son of a milman, Gephardt got his political start as a member of the Board of Aldermen in St. Louis. He was first elected to the U.S. House of Representatives in 1976 and, as chairperson of the House Democratic caucus, is the fourth-ranking Democrat in the lower chamber of Congress. Priding himself on being a consensus builder, he has been an effective leader in legislation on the social security system and tax reform. He also is associated with legislation to require countries that enjoy a large trade surplus with the United States, such as Japan, to open up their markets to U.S. goods. Although personally opposed to abortion, Gephardt changed his position in 1986 so that he no longer favors a constitutional amendment against abortion, on the grounds that it will not solve the problem; he instead favors sex education and family planning as the best means of dealing with the issue. He has campaigned extensively in the neighboring state of Iowa, where he is expected to do well in the caucuses. He also is expected to be the choice of most of the Democratic House members who serve as "superdelegates" to the 1988 convention.

5. Albert Gore, Jr., journalist and home builder, U.S. senator from Tennessee

The son of Albert Gore, who served in the House and Senate for thirty-two years, the junior Gore graduated from Harvard University and attended divinity and law schools before becoming a journalist and subsequently a home builder. He first ran for the House of Representatives in 1976 and served there until he was elected to the Senate in 1984. At thirty-nine, he is the youngest of the Democratic candidates and maintains that he is the only one who actually comes from the baby boom generation of people under forty years of age. A Vietnam veteran, he is particularly interested in nuclear arms control and tries to occupy the middle ground on that issue by favoring reduction rather than elimination of weapons such as the MX missile. Other major issues on which he has concentrated are the environment, the budget deficit, education, and health care. As a southerner, he is expected to do well on Super Tuesday unless white southerners consider him too liberal and opt to vote in the Republican contests held that day.

6. Jesse Jackson, minister, civil rights activist

The only Democratic candidate not to hold public office, Jackson nevertheless was the leader in the polls immediately after Gary Hart withdrew from the race. Jackson considers himself the leader of the "coalition of the rejected," which includes not only blacks but also unemployed shipbuilders, steelworkers, failing farmers, and oil field workers. The most liberal of the candidates, he is highly critical of the moderate wing of the Democrats represented by the Democratic Leadership Council (DLC), which he calls "Democrats for the Leisure Class." A rousing speaker and clever phrase maker, Jackson was criticized during his 1984 Democratic nomination campaign for praising the Palestine Liberation Organization, Fidel Castro of Cuba, and Daniel Ortega of Nicaragua and for failing to disavow the support of black nationalist Louis Farrakhan, considered to be violently anti-Semitic by many Jewish voters. Jackson is expected to do well among blacks, as he did in 1984, a factor that will help him on Super Tuesday.

7. Paul Simon, journalist, U.S. senator from Illinois

As a crusading editor of a small-town newspaper in southern Illinois, Simon ran for a seat in the Illinois House at age twenty-five and went on to serve as an effective legislator in the state Senate. He also served as lieutenant governor of Illinois, and after losing the 1972 gubernatorial primary to a wealthy corporate lawyer, Daniel Walker (who convinced voters that Simon was a tool of Mayor Richard Daley of Chicago), Simon captured a seat in the U.S. House of Representatives in 1974. He served there until he was elected to the Senate in 1984. A disciple of former Illinois senator Paul Douglas and a great admirer of Hubert Humphrey, Simon best represents the traditionally liberal way of the national Democratic party. He is a champion of federal aid to education, including aid for the handicapped, and of relief for world hunger and refuses to take the advice of campaign consultants that he get rid of his bow tie, horned-rim glasses, and liberal political views. His generally strong ties with labor and the proximity of his home base to Iowa are expected to help him in the caucuses there.

Republicans

1. George Bush, businessman, vice president of the United States

Son of former senator Prescott Bush of Connecticut, Bush made a fortune as a drilling contractor in Texas. He was chairperson of the Republican party in Harris County, Texas, and served as a U.S. representative for four years. He lost in two Senate races but has held several high appointive positions including ambassador to the United Nations, chairperson of the Republican National Committee, chief of the U.S. liaison office in Peking, and director of the Central Intelligence Agency. Bush sought the presidential nomination in 1980 but, after winning the Iowa caucuses, lost to Reagan in the New Hampshire primary and in most other states; he withdrew from the race in late May of 1980. Although Reagan and Bush differed on some issues (Bush once referred to supply-side economics as "voodoo economics"), Reagan chose Bush as his running-mate to attract the support of moderate Republicans. Since then the two appear to have worked together effectively; the president has assigned the vice president important responsibilities (including chairing the administration's crisis management team), and Bush has performed his duties faithfully. Nonetheless, many conservatives in the Republican party regard Bush as too moderate and pragmatic; and being vice president, Bush faces the problem of how to be "his own man" while remaining loyal to the president. He is the best financed and best organized of the Republican candidates.

2. Robert Dole, lawyer, U.S. senator from Kansas

Dole served in the Kansas state legislature and as a prosecuting attorney before coming to the House of Representatives in 1961. In 1969 he was elected to the Senate. A former chairperson of the Republican National Committee and the party's vice-presidential candidate in 1976, Dole had a reputation of being a staunch conservative and partisan fighter, with a "hatchet man" image that he furthered during the 1976 campaign. Since then, however, he has changed his behavior and image. In 1980 when he tried for the presidential nomination, Dole avoided personal attacks on his opponents and instead allowed his keen sense of humor (much of it directed against himself) to surface. Although generally conservative, he supports the food stamp program as well as programs for the handicapped. He supported President Reagan's budget and tax cuts in 1981, but as chairperson of the Senate Finance Committee he took the leadership in developing, and getting passed, the $98.3-billion tax increase in 1982. He continues to be highly critical of the budget deficit and of supply-side economics. Despite his concern that social issues threaten to divide the Republican party, he has supported President Reagan on abortion and school prayer, thereby ingratiating himself to conservative Christians. He has been very skillful in calling for full disclosure of the Iran-contra affair without directly criticizing the president.

3. Pierre (Pete) du Pont, lawyer, businessman

Du Pont, formerly governor of Delaware and a member of the wealthy du Pont family, has changed his political views markedly over the years. While serving three terms in the House of Representatives, he compiled a moderate voting record. However, upon being elected governor of Delaware in 1976 when the state had a large budget deficit, a declining economy, and the lowest state bond rating in the country, du Pont initiated a program of major cuts in both taxes and expenditures. When the state economy turned around (with budget surpluses, rapid growth, and one of the highest bond ratings in the nation), du Pont became an avid supply-sider. He now advocates "empowering" people to make more of their own decisions and calls for a private alternative to Social Security, mandatory work programs for welfare recipients, and the elimination of farm price support programs. The first Republican to announce his candidacy publicly, he is considered a long shot for the nomination.

4. Alexander Haig, career military officer, businessman

A career military officer for most of his life, Haig graduated from the U.S. Military Academy, the army and navy war colleges, and Georgetown University, where he received a master's degree in international relations. He served in several executive positions relating to national security affairs before becoming chief of the Nixon White House staff after the resignation of H. R. Haldeman (who was implicated in the Watergate scandal). Haig is credited with influencing President Nixon to resign in August 1974 to avoid the trauma of the impeachment proceedings that would have been instituted against him. In 1974 Haig was appointed commander in chief of the U.S. European Command of the North Atlantic Treaty Organization. He was an early contender for the presidential nomination in 1980 but dropped out of the race and went on to become the first secretary of state in the Reagan administration. While at State, however, he feuded with persons on the White House staff and failed in his attempt to become the "vicar" of foreign policy; in 1982 he was replaced by George Shultz. Supported only by a few obscure members of the military-industrial complex, Haig is given little chance of winning the nomination.

5. Jack Kemp, professional football player, U.S. representative from New York

Known originally as a star quarterback for the Buffalo Bills professional football team, Kemp has long been interested in politics. He was a volunteer in the unsuccessful Nixon and Goldwater presidential campaigns and in Ronald Reagan's successful 1966 campaign for governor of California. He served in the off-season as an assistant to Reagan's chief of staff and in 1970 responded to a search of Erie County Republicans for a strong candidate to win back a congressional seat in suburban Buffalo that they had lost in the 1964 Goldwater debacle. In 1975 he was sold on the idea of supply-side economics by *Wall Street Journal* columnist Jude Wanniski. Kemp spent much of 1977 taking this idea on the road, and soon the national press began to take note of the former quarterback with the missionary zeal. Reagan converted to the theory, embraced the Kemp-Roth plan for a 30 percent, three-year tax cut in his 1980 campaign, and placed Kemp's name on the list of potential running mates. Despite the mounting federal budget deficit, he has remained an avid supply-sider, preaching the message that the U.S. can "grow" itself out of the deficit. An incurable optimist, he enthusiastically supports the Strategic Defense Initiative and advocates bringing traditionally Democratic groups such as minorities, blue-collar workers, and young people into the Republican party.

6. Marion (Pat) Robertson, minister, businessman

Although his father was a well-known senator, Robertson himself, like Jesse Jackson, has never held a public office and is best known as the founder of the Christian Broadcasting Network, a major business operation that generates revenues of more than $200 million a year. Like many businessmen, Robertson is deeply concerned about both the budget and trade deficits. He wants the government to take an active role in enforcing "family values" in such matters as abortion, prayer in the public schools, pornography, and drugs. Like Jackson, he draws into politics a large number of people who otherwise would not participate. Robertson is a highly controversial candidate because he practices faith healing, speaks in tongues, and maintains that he used prayer to change the course of a hurricane. His effort to gather the support of three million people as a condition of his candidacy was running behind schedule in mid-1987, and the problems of the PTL (Praise the Lord) ministry of Jim and Tammy Bakker were taking a toll on Robertson's television ministry, and perhaps his presidential candidacy as well.

Results of Presidential Contests, 1932-1984 ═══ C

Year	Republican nominee (in *italics*) and other major candidates	Democratic nominee (in *italics*) and other major candidates	Election winner	Division of popular vote[a] (percent)	Division of electoral vote[b]
1932	*Herbert Hoover* (incumbent president) Joseph France (former senator from Missouri)	*Franklin D. Roosevelt* (governor of New York) Alfred Smith (former governor of New York) John Garner (representative from Texas and Speaker of the House)	Roosevelt (D)	57-40	472-59
1936	*Alfred Landon* (governor of Kansas) William Borah (senator from Idaho)	*Franklin D. Roosevelt* (incumbent president) None	Roosevelt (D)	61-37	523-8
1940	*Wendell Willkie* (Indiana lawyer and public utility executive) Thomas E. Dewey (U.S. district attorney for New York) Robert Taft (senator from Ohio)	*Franklin D. Roosevelt* (incumbent president) None	Roosevelt (D)	55-45	449-82
1944	*Thomas E. Dewey* (governor of New York) Wendell Willkie (previous Republican presidential nominee)	*Franklin D. Roosevelt* (incumbent president) Harry Byrd (senator from Virginia)	Roosevelt (D)	53-46	432-99

Year					
1948	Thomas E. Dewey (governor of New York) Harold Stassen (former governor of Minnesota) Robert Taft (senator from Ohio)	Harry S Truman (incumbent president) Richard Russell (senator from Georgia)	Truman (D)	50-45	303-189
1952	Dwight D. Eisenhower (general) Robert Taft (senator from Ohio)	Adlai Stevenson (governor of Illinois) Estes Kefauver (senator from Tennessee) Richard Russell (senator from Georgia)	Eisenhower (R)	55-44	442-89
1956	Dwight D. Eisenhower (incumbent president) None	Adlai Stevenson (previous Democratic presidential nominee) Averell Harriman (governor of New York)	Eisenhower (R)	57-42	457-73
1960	Richard Nixon (vice president) None	John F. Kennedy (senator from Massachusetts) Hubert Humphrey (senator from Minnesota) Lyndon B. Johnson (senator from Texas)	Kennedy (D)	49.7-49.5	303-219
1964	Barry Goldwater (senator from Arizona) Nelson Rockefeller (governor of New York)	Lyndon B. Johnson (incumbent president) None	Johnson (D)	61-39	486-52

Year	Republican nominee (in italics) and other major candidates	Democratic nominee (in italics) and other major candidates	Election winner	Division of popular vote[a] (percent)	Division of electoral vote[b]
1968	*Richard Nixon* (former Republican presidential nominee) Ronald Reagan (governor of California)	*Hubert Humphrey* (incumbent vice president) Robert F. Kennedy (senator from New York) Eugene McCarthy (senator from Minnesota)	Nixon (R)	43.4-42.7	301-191
1972	*Richard Nixon* (incumbent president) None	*George McGovern* (senator from South Dakota) Hubert Humphrey (senator from Minnesota) George Wallace (governor of Alabama)	Nixon (R)	61-38	520-17
1976	*Gerald R. Ford* (incumbent president) Ronald Reagan (former governor of California)	*Jimmy Carter* (former governor of Georgia) Edmund Brown, Jr. (governor of California) George Wallace (governor of Alabama)	Carter (D)	50-48	297-240
1980	*Ronald Reagan* (former governor of California) George Bush (former director of Central Intelligence Agency) John Anderson (representative from Illinois)	*Jimmy Carter* (incumbent president) Edward M. Kennedy (senator from Massachusetts)	Reagan (R)	51-41	489-49

| 1984 | Ronald Reagan (incumbent president) None | Walter F. Mondale (former vice president) Gary Hart (senator from Colorado) | Reagan (R) | 59-41 | 525-13 |

a Division of popular vote is between the Republican and Democratic nominees.
b Division of electoral votes is between the Republican and Democratic nominees.

Index

Abortion issues, 42, 56
Abramson, Paul, 97
Acceptance speeches, 55
Adams, John, 7
Adams, John Quincy, 8, 123
Advertising, 78-80, 83
AFL-CIO (American Federation of
  Labor and Congress of Industrial
  Organizations), 33, 47, 56, 85-86, 125
Agnew, Spiro, 100
Alaskan natives, 93
Aldrich, John, 97
Alexander, Herbert, 20
American Bar Association, 125
American Farm Bureau, 124
American Indians, 14, 93
Anderson, John, 32, 37, 42, 43, 80, 122
Anti-Mason party, 8
Asher, Herbert, 104
Asian-Americans, 93
Askew, Reubin, 32, 42
Automatic plan, 124, 125

Babbitt, Bruce, 23, 33, 135
Baker, Howard, 23, 32
Baker, Russell, 31
Bandwagon technique, 52-53
Barkley, Alben, 24
Biden, Joseph, 23, 135-136
Braun, Alan, 127
Broder, David, 44, 57
Brokaw, Tom, 44
Brown, Edmund (Jerry), 17, 25, 26,
  31, 32

Buchanan, James, 39
Buckley, William F., 33
Buckley v. Valeo, 18
Burnham, Walter Dean, 112
Burr, Aaron, 62
Bush, George, 25, 54, 138-139
  campaign finance, 32, 47
  election politics, 74, 81
  nomination politics, 34, 42, 43
Byrne, Jane, 46, 72

California, 19, 65
California primary, 15, 17, 36, 37, 50
Campaign promises, 51, 115
Campaigns. *See* Election campaigns;
  Nomination campaigns
Campbell, Angus, 109
Candidates
  debates, 33, 43, 44, 80-81, 121, 122
  image, 42, 72-74
  personal characteristics, 25-27
  political experience, 21-25
  qualifications, 20-21
  voter reactions to, 101-109
Carter, Jimmy, 15, 110, 115
  background, 21-23, 25
  election politics, 67, 69-70, 72,
    73, 76-82, 84, 86, 87, 122, 123,
    127
  nomination politics, 17, 24, 30-34,
    36, 43, 45-47, 52, 54, 55
  voter response to, 101, 108, 114
Carter-Mondale Presidential
  Committee, 87

Index

Caucuses
  caucus-conventions, 12, 38, 45-46,
    120
  congressional caucuses, 7-8, 119
  delegate caucuses, 56
Chamber of Commerce, 125
Church, Frank, 23, 54
Citizens for the Republic, 32
Civil rights issues, 106
Clay, Henry, 8
Cleveland, Grover, 123
Commission on Campaign Costs, 18
Committee to Reelect the President,
  72, 75, 84
Common Cause, 87
Congressional caucuses, 7-8, 119
Connally, John, 32, 37, 42, 47
Consultants, 49
Converse, Philip, 98, 100
Crane, Philip, 32, 42
Cranston, Alan, 32, 33, 42, 42
Crawford, William, 8
Credentials contests, 50
Crisis mentality, 39

Davis, Richard, 82
Dealignment politics, 112-113
Debates, 33, 43, 44, 80-81, 121, 122
"Decomposition" politics, 112
Delegates
  allocation, 10-11
  caucuses, 56
  selection, 11-17, 120
  superdelegates, 15, 16, 120
Democratic National Committee, 13,
  15, 16, 51
Democratic party, 27 n.3
  constituency, 74, 101
  delegate allocation, 10-11
  delegate selection, 9, 12-16
Democratic-Republican party, 8, 27
  n.3
Deviating election, 110, 115
Dewey, Thomas, 21, 53, 123
Direct-mail specialists, 49
Direct national primary, 127-128
Direct popular election, 60, 125-128
Disclosure of financial information,
  19
District of Columbia, 94

District plan, 124, 125
Dole, Robert, 23, 25, 32, 42, 72, 116
  n.5, 139
Dukakis, Michael, 23, 136
du Pont, Pierre (Pete), 25, 33, 139

Eagleton, Thomas, 54, 55
Economic issues, 76, 108
Education levels of voters, 97-98
Eisenhower, Dwight D., 21, 23, 50, 73,
  77, 93, 104, 110, 115
Election campaigns, 59
  candidate debates, 80-81, 121, 122
  finance, 66-67, 85, 86, 122
  function of, 1-2
  length, 57, 67
  locality of first speech, 67
  manipulating political appeals, 70-
    78
  media coverage, 83
  media use, 78-81
  nomination campaign compared,
    29-30
  organization and workers, 83-86
  targeting of campaign efforts, 68-70
Elections
  characteristics of U.S. elections, 2
  effect on party system, 109-113
  effect on policy making, 113-116
  function of, 1-2
Electoral college, 4 n.5, 6, 68, 91
  mechanism, 60-66
  reform, 122-128
Electorate, 5, 39
Ellsworth, Robert, 69
Emerson, Ralph Waldo, 73
Equal Rights Amendment (ERA), 42,
  56, 115
Equal-time requirement, 89 n.21
Ethnic groups, 14, 65

Fairness Commission, 15-16
Federal Communications Act of 1934,
  89 n.21
Federal Election Commission (FEC),
  19, 66, 87
Federal grants, 39, 46
Federalist Papers, The, 61
Federalist party, 6-7, 62
Ferraro, Geraldine, 54, 74, 75, 81, 82

Fifteenth Amendment, 92, 93
Financing
  election campaigns, 66-67, 85, 86,
    122
  nomination campaigns, 18-20, 32,
    47-49, 120
"Firing Line," 33
Florida primary, 37
Ford, Gerald R., 24
  election politics, 67, 71-73, 76, 79,
    80, 82-84, 86, 123, 127
  nomination politics, 37, 38, 51, 52,
    56
Fowler, Donald L., 16
Future of America, 32

Garagiola, Joe, 79, 86
Gasoline import fee, 42
Georgia primary, 37
Gephardt, Richard A., 23, 33, 136-137
Germond, Jack, 44
Ginn Committee, 16
Glenn, John, 42, 46, 54
Goldwater, Barry, 115
  background, 22, 25, 26
  election politics, 71, 74, 85
  nomination politics, 36, 46, 51, 53,
    55
  voter response to, 101, 110
Gore, Albert, Jr., 23, 137
Gossett, Ed, 124
Governors
  office, as precursor to presidency,
    21-23
  role in delegate selection, 11, 16, 56
Graham, Katharine, 31
Grovey v. Townsend, 93
Guinn v. United States, 93
Gun control, 42

Hadley, Arthur, 30
Haig, Alexander, 25, 140
Hamilton, Alexander, 6, 61, 62
*Harper v. Virginia State Board of
  Elections,* 116 n.4
Harris, Fred, 20
Harrison, Benjamin, 123
Hart, Gary, 15, 18, 42, 84
  nomination politics, 32-34, 37, 42,
    43, 44, 45, 49, 52, 120

Hatch Act of 1940, 18
Hayes, Rutherford B., 123
Heclo, Hugh, 5
Hess, Stephen, 1
Hispanics, 93
Hollings, Ernest, 32, 43
Hoover, Herbert, 24, 76
House of Representatives, 61, 63, 123
Humphrey, Hubert H., 71
  election politics, 64, 69, 71-72, 77,
    84, 85, 123
  nomination politics, 12, 15, 17, 24,
    46, 50, 55
  social background, 25, 26
Hunt Commission, 15
Hyman, Sidney, 25

Illinois primary, 37
Incumbency, advantage of, 23, 24, 38-
  39, 46, 71-72
Independent voters, 99-100
Inflation, 108
Information, disclosure of, 19
Interest groups, 47, 56
International Association of
  Machinists and Aerospace Workers,
  47
Invisible primary, 30
Iowa caucuses, 30, 38, 45, 121
Iran hostage crisis, 39
Issues, importance to voters, 42, 76-
  78, 106-109

Jackson, Andrew, 8, 123
Jackson, Henry, 23, 37, 71
Jackson, Jesse, 15, 18, 23, 34, 43, 52,
  75, 84, 137
Jay Treaty, 6
Jefferson, Thomas, 6-8, 62
Jennings, Peter, 44
Johnson, Lady Bird, 79
Johnson, Lyndon B., 23, 77, 93
  background, 24, 25
  nomination politics, 54, 55
  voter response to, 101, 104,
    115
Jordan, Hamilton, 69-70, 84

Kefauver, Estes, 23, 24
Kemp, Jack F., 25, 33, 140

Kennedy, Edward M., 26, 72, 79, 86
  nomination politics, 17, 31-34, 37-
    43, 45-47, 51, 52, 55
Kennedy, Jacqueline, 83
Kennedy, Joan, 31
Kennedy, John F., 18, 124
  background, 22, 25, 26
  election politics, 64, 69, 70, 73, 77,
    80, 83, 84, 115, 123
  nomination politics, 31, 36, 37, 54,
    55
  public response to, 104
Kennedy, Robert F., 24-26, 54, 84
Kessel, John, 84
Key, V. O., 115
Khrushchev, Nikita, 70
Kirk, Paul G., Jr., 16
Kirkpatrick, Jeane, 46
Kissinger, Henry, 27 n.14
Koch, Edward, 46
Kopechne, Mary Jo, 31, 45
Kraft, Tim, 30

Landon, Alfred, 21
LaRouche, Lyndon, 32
League of Women Voters, 80
Legal qualifications for presidency,
  20
Lincoln, Abraham, 127
Literacy tests, 92, 93
Lodge, Henry Cabot, 124
Longley, Lawrence, 64, 65, 127

McCarthy, Eugene J., 127
  background, 26
  election politics, 71, 84
  nomination politics, 23, 24, 36, 46,
    55
McCormack, Ellen, 20
McGovern, George
  background, 22, 25, 26, 43
  election politics, 69, 71, 77-78, 84,
    85
  nomination politics, 9-10, 15, 17,
    30, 34, 36, 37, 42, 46, 50, 54, 55
  voter response to, 101, 104
McGovern Commission, 10, 13, 14
Madison, James, 6, 8, 60
Maine, 124
Maintaining election, 109-110, 115

Mandate, 113, 115
Mason, George, 60
Massachusetts primary, 37
Matthews, Donald, 33
Meany, George, 55, 85
Media
  coverage of election campaign, 81-
    83
  coverage of nomination process, 44-
    45, 56-57, 121
  influence, 31, 33, 49
  televised debates, 43, 44, 80-81, 121
  television commercials, 33, 43, 78-
    80
Media consultants, 49
Medicaid funds, 56
"Meet the Press," 31, 39
Miami Herald, 33
Michigan Center for Political
  Studies, 104
Michigan primary, 34, 37
Mikulski Commission, 13, 14
Miller, Arthur, 108
Miller, Warren, 108, 114
Minority groups
  as convention delegates, 14, 16, 56
  voter turnout, 97
  voting rights, 93-94
Mitchell, John, 84
Mondale, Walter F., 111
  background, 25, 26, 43
  election politics, 69, 70, 74-81, 84-
    86
  nomination politics, 17-18, 30, 32-
    34, 37, 42, 43, 44, 45, 47, 52, 54,
    120
  voter response to, 101, 105-106,
    108, 109, 114
Monroe, James, 8
Montana primary, 16
Morris, Gouverneur, 60
Mudd, Roger, 31, 45
Muskie, Edmund, 31, 46, 54

National bonus plan, 125, 126
National conventions
  balloting process, 52-53
  credentials contests, 50
  delegate allocation, 10-11
  delegate caucuses, 56

delegate selection, 11-18, 120
effect of direct popular elections
  on, 127-128
evolution of, 8-9, 119
fights over rules, 51
location, 50
media role, 56-57
party platforms, 51-52
recent changes, 55-57
rules and politics of, 50-55
show of party unity, 55
superdelegates, 15, 16, 120
vice-presidential nominee
  selection, 53-55
welcoming speech, 50
National Education Association
  (NEA), 33, 47, 56, 86
National Organization of Women, 33
National primary, 127-128
National Public Radio, 83
National Republican party, 8
Native Americans, 14, 93
New Hampshire primary, 23, 36, 38,
  121
New York primary, 37
Newsweek magazine, 83
Nimmo, Dan, 83
Nineteenth Amendment, 94
Nixon, Richard, 76, 110
  background, 24-26
  election politics, 64, 69-72, 74, 77,
    78, 80, 83, 84, 115, 123
  nomination politics, 20, 31, 52
  voter response to, 101, 104, 114
Nomination campaigns
  campaign workers, 30-31, 45-47
  candidate debates, 43, 44
  caucus-conventions, 12, 38, 45-46,
    120
  election campaign compared, 29-30
  financing, 18-20, 32, 47-49, 120
  initial strategies, 30-34
  interaction of strategic factors, 49-
    50
  labor endorsements, 33
  manipulating political appeals, 38-
    42
  media role, 31, 43, 44-45
  national convention, 8-9, 50-57
  "popularity" contests, 32-33

spending limits, 34, 47
See also Presidential primaries
Nomination process
  current nomination rules, 9-20
  delegate allocation, 10-11
  delegate selection, 11-18
  effect of direct popular elections
    on, 127-128
  evolution of process, 2, 5-9, 119-121

PACs. *See* Political action
  committees
Parliamentary government, 2
Parties. *See* Political parties
Patterson, Thomas, 44, 82
Pennsylvania primary, 37
Personal characteristics of
  candidates, 25-27
Personal image, 42
Phillips, Kevin, 112
Pierce, Franklin, 39
Playboy magazine, 83
Pokorny, Eugene, 30
Policy making, 113-116
Political action committees, 18, 66
Political backgrounds of candidates,
  21-25
Political consultants, 49
Political parties
  consequences of presidential
    elections on, 109-113
  effect of direct popular elections
    on, 126-127
  historical background, 6-7
  party affiliation, 98-100
  party labels, 38, 70-71
  party leaders, 11, 17, 31, 46, 56, 120,
    126, 127
  platforms, 51-52, 128
Poll taxes, 92, 93
Pollsters, 49
Pomper, Gerald, 106, 113
"Popularity" contests, 32-33
Position issues, 42, 76-78, 106-109
Presidential office, requirements, 20-
  27
Presidential primaries, 11-12, 119-121
  direct national primary, 127-128
  strategies for, 34, 36-38

"winner-take-all" issue, 14-15, 17, 45
"winner-take-more" principle, 27 n.9
Profiles in Courage (Kennedy), 31
Property qualifications, 63, 92
Proportional plan, 124, 125
Public opinion polls, 49

Quota system for delegate selection, 14

Racial discrimination, 92-94
Racial unrest, 100
Radio influence, 83
Rafshoon, Gerald, 84
Ranney, Austin, 20, 29, 127
Rather, Dan, 44
Reagan, Nancy, 79
Reagan, Ronald
  background, 21-23, 25-26
  election politics, 65, 67, 69-82, 84-87, 122
  1980 election outcome, 110-111, 115
  1984 election outcome, 111
  nomination politics, 31-34, 37, 38, 42, 43, 46, 47, 51-54, 57
  public response to, 101, 105-106, 108-109, 114
Realigning election, 110-113, 116
Reedy, George, 115
Reinstating election, 117 n.38
Republican National Committee, 17
Republican party (contemporary), 25
  constituency, 101
  delegate allocation, 10
  delegate selection, 16-17
Republican party (early), 6-7, 62
Residence requirements, 94
Retrospective voting, 114
Robertson, Marion G. (Pat), 25, 141
Robinson, Michael, 82
Roche, John, 62
Rockefeller, Nelson, 24, 26, 51, 53
Rohde, David, 97
Roll call vote, 52
Romney, George, 27 n.14, 51, 73
Roosevelt, Franklin D., 21, 52, 54, 93
Russell, Richard, 24

Schumpeter, Joseph, 1
Schweiker, Richard, 51
Selectorate, 5, 29, 34, 39, 42
Senate
  office, as precursor to presidency, 21-22
  role in selection of vice president, 63
Shafer, Byron, 119, 120
Sheehan, Margaret, 82
Sherman, Roger, 60
Shriver, Sargent, 71
Simon, Paul, 23
Six Crises (Nixon), 31
Slogans, 76, 77
Smith v. Allwright, 93
Social group dynamics, 74-75, 97-98, 101-102
Spending limits, 34, 47, 67, 86
Split-level realignment, 112
Split-ticket voting, 99-100
State conventions, 11, 119
States' Rights party, 51
Steiger, William, 17
Stevenson, Adlai, 24, 50, 53, 54, 104
Stevenson, Adlai III, 55
Stone, W. Clement, 20
Strauss, Robert, 84
Suffrage. *See* Voter turnout
Superdelegates, 15, 16, 120

Taft, Robert A., 50
Taft-Hartley Act, 18
Teamsters union, 86
Television. *See* Media
Thurmond, J. Strom, 51, 66
Tilden, Samuel, 123
Truman, Harry S, 23, 24, 70, 71, 93, 123
Turner, Terry, 31
Twelfth Amendment, 62-63
Twentieth Century Fund, 125
Twenty-fourth Amendment, 93
Twenty-second Amendment, 23
Twenty-sixth Amendment, 94
Twenty-third Amendment, 94

Udall, Morris, 26, 37
Unions
  campaign contributions, 18

campaign work, 85-86
candidate endorsement, 33, 47, 86

Valence issues, 89 n.19
Van Buren, Martin, 8
Vice-presidential office
  nominee selection, 53-55, 127
  as precursor to presidency, 23-24
  responsibilities, 24
Vietnam War, 100, 106
Voter registration, 86
Voter turnout
  equality of suffrage rights, 63, 91-
  94
  influence of issues, events, and
    presidential performance, 106-109
  party affiliation effects, 98-100
  reactions to candidates, 102-106
  social group differences, 97-98, 101-
  102
  trends, 94-97
Voting Rights Act of 1965, 93-94

Walesa, Stanislaw, 75
Wallace, George, 85, 123

Wallace, Henry, 54, 66
Washington, George, 6
Watergate affair, 100
Weicker, Lowell, 34
Welcoming speech, 50
West Virginia primary, 37
Whig party, 27 n.7
Why Not the Best? (Carter), 31
Wicker, Tom, 31
Willkie, Wendell, 21
Wilson, James, 60
Winograd Commission, 13, 51
Wisconsin primary, 16, 37
Witcover, Jules, 44
Women
  as convention delegates, 14, 16, 17,
  56
  political issues, 75
  suffrage extended to, 94
  voter turnout, 97

Young people, 14, 16, 75
  as convention delegates, 14, 16
  political issues, 75
  suffrage extended to, 94
  voter turnout, 97